WILLIAMS · SONOMA

Celebrating the
Pleasures of Cooking

WILLIAMS · SONOMA

Celebrating the
Pleasures of Cooking

By

CHUCK WILLIAMS

General Editor

NORMAN KOLPAS

TIME-LIFE BOOKS
Time-Life Books is a division of Time Life Inc.
Time-Life is a trademark of Time Warner Inc. U.S.A.

TIME-LIFE CUSTOM PUBLISHING
Vice President and Publisher: Terry Newell
Director of New Product Development: Quentin McAndrew
Managing Editor: Donia Ann Steele
Director of Sales: Neil Levin
Director of Financial Operations: J. Brian Birky

WILLIAMS-SONOMA
Founder/Vice Chairman: Chuck Williams
Book Buyer: Victoria Kalish

WELDON OWEN, INC.
President: John Owen
Vice President and Publisher: Wendely Harvey
Chief Financial Officer: Larry Partington
Editor: Hannah Rahill
General Editor: Norman Kolpas
Copy Editor: Sharon Silva
Proofreader: Sharilyn Hovind
Proofreader/Indexer: Ken DellaPenta
Design: Kari Perin, Perin + Perin
Layout Production: Kristen Wurz
Production Director: Stephanie Sherman
Production Manager: Jen Dalton
Food Photographer: Allan Rosenberg
Memorabilia Photography: Allen V. Lott
Food Stylist: Heidi Gintner
Assistant Food Stylist: Kim Konecny
Cover and Chapter Opener Photography: Karl Petzke Photography
Cover and Chapter Opener Food Stylist: Sandra Cook

A Weldon Owen Production
Copyright © 1997 Weldon Owen Inc.

Library of Congress Cataloging-in-Publication Data

Williams, Chuck.
    Williams-Sonoma's celebrating the pleasures of cooking:
Chuck Williams commemorates 40 years of cooking in America/
general editor. Norman Kolpas.
        p.   cm.
    Includes index.
    ISBN 0-7835-4934-2
    1. Cookery.   2. Cookery—United States—History
    I. Kolpas, Norman.   II. Title.
TX714.W5234   1997
641.5973—dc21   97-5712
                    CIP

10 9 8 7 6 5 4 3 2 1

Manufactured by Toppan Printing Co., (H.K.) Ltd.
Printed in China

CONTENTS

"Good cooking transforms the satisfying of a basic need into one of man's greatest pleasures."

–Nicholas Roosevelt, *Good Cooking* (1959)

THERE IS A GOOD, SIMPLE REASON why this book is called *Celebrating the Pleasures of Cooking*. Those words, in a nutshell, sum up what both Williams-Sonoma and I have been about for 40 years: giving people pleasure.

Each chapter examines the cooking trends I observed during a particular decade of Williams-Sonoma's history. Yet, I don't want to give you the impression that my observations, or the recipes with which I illustrate them, pretend in any way to reflect what America as a whole has been cooking since 1956.

For its first 16 years of business, Williams-Sonoma remained a single store with a clientele of people who loved to cook. Our customers came only from a small segment of the population, largely urban people who probably traveled to Europe on vacation and who, if they didn't live in the San Francisco area, visited often. During the last 24 years, however, that situation has changed dramatically, and American cooking has changed with it. Just as we grew from one and then a handful of stores to the more than 150 shops across the country, so was there an explosion in America's interest in cooking and serving fine food, both in the home and in restaurants.

These developments can be explained in terms of societal and economic trends, of course, both of which I touch on in each of the four chapter introductions. But I would rather focus on the people who led us on our journeys of discovery, such as Dione Lucas, Michael Field, James Beard, Julia Child, Marcella Hazan, Elizabeth David, Richard Olney and countless other cookbook authors, chefs and cooking teachers.

Perhaps the best way to sum up the changes I have seen over the past 40 years is to look at our attitude toward bread, that most basic of foods. Back in the 1950s, most Americans were eating mass-produced, fluffy, flavorless, presliced white bread. We had lost the art of bread making as our

grandmothers had done it. By the early 1960s, however, Paula Peck had produced the excellent *The Art of Fine Baking* (1961) and Elizabeth David had shown us how easy it could be to make a good round country loaf (page 45) in the European style. Our senses awakened to the possibilities, we grew more serious and bolder and in 1970 attempted Julia Child's 20-page-long recipe with detailed instructions for the classic French breads in volume two of her *Mastering the Art of French Cooking*.

In 1978, during Williams-Sonoma's third decade, a dedicated American cooking teacher and author brought us down-to-earth instructions for everyday baking in *Bernard Clayton's Bread Book*. Later in that decade, the arrival of French bread bakeries and Il Fornaio, a high-quality Italian bakery, showed us how good fresh-baked European bread could be. Our fourth decade saw the arrival of the countertop electric bread machine, which put the pleasures of hot, fresh, home-baked bread easily within anyone's reach.

Over 40 years we have progressed, in short, from a diminishing knowledge of fundamental cooking to early infatuations with French and Italian cooking, from ambitious attempts at mastering complicated preparations to accepting the simpler joys of cooking as part of our daily lives. What has not changed, however, is the joy we take in sharing the pleasures of cooking with others. I am pleased that this book gives me the chance to share with you the recipes that have brought me the most pleasure over the past 40 years.

Williams-Sonoma gave me the chance to get to know some of the greatest cookbook authors of our time, including Julia Child (left), James Beard (right, in my home kitchen) and Elizabeth David (at Il Fornaio).

The Start of a Tradition

MANY OF OUR CUSTOM-ERS have long known how Williams-Sonoma got its start and grew. If you haven't, here is the story.

After working overseas for four years on American air bases during World War II, I eventually wound up living in the California wine country town of Sonoma. That was where, as a self-taught carpenter, I built a house from the ground up, finishing it in 1947 and getting my general contractor's license as a result. I went on building houses, and when a hardware store near the Sonoma town square came up for sale in 1954, it seemed like a good opportunity to do something else as well.

During those years, I was part of a group of friends who loved to cook and eat together, and we experimented with the best in classic French and traditional American cooking. I had also taken a trip to Paris, Brussels and Copenhagen in 1952, and was

instantly consumed with their wonderful food and excellent cookware, bakeware and tools. Soon I was carrying a few professional-quality pots and pans and cooking tools in my hardware store along with the nuts and bolts and cans of redwood stain. My continued fascination with what I had seen in Europe eventually pushed the hardware out of the store. By 1956, Williams-Sonoma as people know it today was created in one small part of the building, right down to the now-familiar open display shelves and cabinets I first designed and built.

That original Williams-Sonoma store gained such a following among Bay Area cooks that, two years later, with the help of my friend Mike Sharp, I was convinced to close up shop in Sonoma and move lock, stock and barrel to Sutter Street in San Francisco. At the beginning, it was just the two of us, with Wade Bentson adding his help and talent a few years later. The first few months convinced me to make the first yearly trip to Paris to find merchandise

WILLIAMS-SONOMA

to fill the shop. The shop became a must-see for anyone who was visiting the city and interested in cooking, especially French cooking. In walked such greats of American cooking as James Beard, Helen Evans Brown, Julia Child and others.

In 1971, with the encouragement of Edward Marcus of Neiman-Marcus and the help of Jackie Mallorca, we created our first professional mail-order catalog, which has gone on to become an important part of the business. Williams-Sonoma remained just one store until 1973, when we opened our Beverly Hills branch; that was followed by Palo Alto in 1974 and Costa Mesa the year after that. In 1978, Howard Lester acquired the company and led us in an expansion that saw us go public, and today we are a large company of stores and catalogs.

Throughout this period of incredible growth, I have stayed creatively involved in the business, still traveling in search of

the best cookware, bakeware and specialty food products to bring to our customers. From the very beginning, I have collected, developed, tested and written recipes both for the stores and catalogs. Many of these recipes are included in this book. My life's purpose has remained the same since the moment Williams-Sonoma opened 40 years ago: to share with others the pleasures of cooking.

1956–1966
FRIENDS WHO LOVE TO COOK

Social historians might tell you that the most important thing that happened in American cooking during the 1950s was the way our postwar prosperity and busy lives led to the development of convenience foods, how things like frozen TV dinners and zippy can openers became the rage. That may be so. But from my point of view, living in the wine country town of Sonoma, close to San Francisco, very different developments were under way: a growing awareness of French cuisine and a renewed interest in honest home cooking using fresh ingredients. Both trends supported the early years of Williams-Sonoma and are reflected in the recipes I've chosen for this chapter.

In Sonoma in the 1950s, I became friends with a small group of people who loved to cook for one another. The group was informally led by a Frenchwoman, Thérèse Bacon, along with our good friend, Ola Tryon. In her old two-story house, Ola had an enormous room with a huge stone fireplace at one end, a beautiful, large

brass-trimmed black restaurant stove at the other, and a 16-foot long French farmhouse kitchen table in the center. It was a truly wonderful room and the center of much of our cooking. In those postwar years, travel was cheap and people were beginning to visit France. That literally fed their interest in soufflés, omelets, onion soup and all those other bistro-style dishes that I tasted there myself on my earliest trips.

The interest in French cooking was also fed by some marvelous cookbooks. We all read and cooked from *Gourmet* magazine, and then from *The Gourmet Cookbook,* which the editors had first brought out in 1950. The magazine published a column on French cooking by chef Louis Diat, whose recipes were posthumously collected in 1960 in *The Gourmet Basic French Cookbook.* We were becoming acquainted with real French cooking through the intelligent writings of an Englishwoman, Elizabeth David, who wrote *A Book of Mediterranean Food* (1950) and *French Country Cooking* (1951), both of which were first published in the United States in 1958. In 1961, Joseph Donon, a master French chef and the Vanderbilt family cook for 38 years, came out with *The Classic French Cuisine,* in which he interpreted classic French recipes for the American home cook.

And, of course, there was Julia Child. She, along with her then-partners Simone Beck and Louisette Bertholle, brought out the first volume of *Mastering the Art of French Cooking* in 1961, three years after I'd moved the store to San Francisco. But Julia really caught on in the years after she debuted on television in 1963 as "The French Chef." She was perhaps the single most influential presence in American cooking at that time. I didn't even need to watch her show to know what she'd cooked on any given night because the next morning countless customers would come into our store to ask for exactly the same-size charlotte mold or sauté pan that Julia had used.

French cuisine wasn't the only cooking my friends and customers were doing during this decade. In recent years, food writers and chefs have made a big deal about California cuisine, as if it were a new development. I can tell you that in the 1950s in the wine country, the Bay Area, Pasadena, Beverly Hills and Santa Barbara, California cooking was already happening. Cooks made imaginative use of the fresh seafood and excellent produce that the geography and climate afforded them. Since the 1930s and before, Japanese-American farmers and home gardeners had grown artichokes and fresh herbs and pencil-thin green asparagus, things you didn't see elsewhere in the country. Helen Evans Brown, an Easterner who moved to Pasadena, discovered the bounty of unusual ingredients available and included them in her recipe column for the then-famous Jurgenson food store of Pasadena and Beverly Hills. She wrote *The West Coast Cook Book* back in 1952. I felt fortunate to have finally met this marvelous cook in 1959 as she died soon after.

Good American cooking also held our interest, as it continues to do today. I enjoyed some cookbooks by writers who didn't pretend to be anything other than who they were. Craig Claiborne, legendary food editor of the *New York Times,* set a high standard with the first edition of his *New York Times Cookbook* in 1960. Peggy Harvey, a society woman with a down-to-earth style, wrote a couple of wonderful works, including *Season to Taste* in 1960, which gave a practical American twist even to dishes she'd learned while studying at Cordon Bleu in Paris. I believe that, had she not died at a young age, everyone who loves good food and cookbooks would know her name today.

One American name that endures is that of James Beard, who celebrated honest American food in a shelf full of cookbooks, including *The James Beard Cookbook,* published in 1959. I believe Jim first visited Williams-Sonoma less than a year after we opened in San Francisco. A man of enormous appetites for both food and friendship, he introduced lots of people to the store. He also introduced me in the early 1960s to Elizabeth David, who became a great friend and, for a while, even wrote a newsletter and informative little pamphlets for us.

Such personal relationships are my fondest memories from that first decade. They enrich virtually every recipe on the following pages.

There were a growing awareness of French cuisine and a renewed interest in honest home cooking using fresh ingredients.

While the only tools you need to prepare the recipe at right are common ones, true lovers of asparagus can find several items that are specially made for its preparation and eating. The small, chrome-plated steel asparagus peeler (below) grips an individual spear while its black

steel swivel-ing blade strips off the tough portion of the peel. An asparagus steamer is a tall, cylindrical pot with a perforated inner pot or basket and a lid. It is designed to hold asparagus upright, allowing the thick stalks to boil in the water while the more tender tips cook in the rising steam. And little silver asparagus tongs (below) allow each guest to pick up and eat individual spears. The tongs were all the rage in elegant res-taurants in the 1950s in France, where I remember seeing them in the dining room of the Plaza Athénée hotel in Paris.

ASPARAGUS WITH HOLLANDAISE SAUCE

SERVES 4

In most of the country, before the 1950s, nearly the only asparagus you could find in markets was white asparagus. The spears had been blanched by piling dirt around them as they grew to shield them from the sun and stop their chlorophyll from developing. However, I remember that gardeners in Sonoma in the 1950s were growing asparagus that they allowed to turn green in the sun, and people discovered how good the spears tasted and how pretty they looked with a rich, creamy, golden hollandaise sauce.

FOR THE HOLLANDAISE SAUCE:
2 egg yolks
1 tablespoon fresh lemon juice
6 tablespoons (3 oz) unsalted butter, at room temperature,
  cut into small cubes
salt and white pepper

1½ lb asparagus
2 teaspoons salt
1 orange

TO MAKE THE HOLLANDAISE, place the egg yolks and lemon juice in a heatproof bowl or the top pan of a double boiler. Set the bowl or pan over (but not touching) simmering water in a saucepan or the bottom pan of the double boiler. Whisk together the egg yolks and the lemon juice until warm and just beginning to thicken, about 1 minute. While continuing to whisk, add the butter a little at a time until all of it is incorporated and the sauce has thickened, 2–3 minutes. (Do not cook the mixture too long or the eggs will curdle.) Remove the bowl or pan from over the water to stop the cooking, and season the sauce to taste with salt and white pepper. Stir in a little water if the sauce is too thick. To keep the sauce warm until the asparagus is cooked, place the bowl or pan, covered, over warm water off the heat. You should have about ¾ cup sauce.

CUT OR BREAK OFF any tough white ends of the asparagus spears. Trim all the spears to the same length. If the spears are large, peel the tough outer skins from them as well: Using a vegetable peeler and starting 2 inches below the tip, peel off the thin outer skin.

SELECT A SAUTÉ PAN or frying pan large enough to hold the asparagus flat in a single layer and fill half full with water. Place over high heat and bring to a boil. Add the salt and asparagus (the water should just cover the asparagus) and return to a boil. Reduce the heat slightly and boil gently, uncovered, until the spears are tender but still crisp, 6–9 minutes, depending upon their size. Drain well.

TO SERVE, arrange the asparagus on warmed individual plates and spoon the warm hollandaise sauce in a crosswise band over the middle of the spears. Holding the orange over each serving and using a zester or fine-holed shredder, shred a little orange zest directly over the sauce. Serve immediately. ✾

I REMEMBER
reading in Gourmet *magazine that German Elector Karl Theodor (1724–99), who lived in the castle at Schwetzingen, an area generally conceded to be the best asparagus-growing region in Germany, liked his asparagus cooked in Champagne. I say the Elector can keep his sparkling wine. I would rather eat my asparagus served on toast with copious quantities of melted clarified butter, which falls into the toast along with the vegetable's essence. If you can bear to wait, garnish each portion with sieved hard-cooked egg white and crossed strips of pimiento.*

17

Sliced Cucumber Salad

This perfectly simple little recipe is typical of the salads you'd find in French bistros in the 1950s. Peel and slice a young cucumber (preferably the English hothouse variety). Combine 1 tablespoon white wine vinegar, 1 teaspoon lemon juice and 2 tablespoons sugar. Stir until dissolved. Pour over the cucumber slices and turn the slices until all are coated. Let stand for 5–10 minutes, then serve.

CELERI-RAVE REMOULADE

SERVES 4

A French bistro dish I fell in love with in the 1950s and still order whenever I see it on a menu, this classic salad of shredded celeriac in a creamy dressing flavored with Dijon mustard and lemon juice captured the attention of many Americans in the early 1960s. If you like, use ½ cup bottled mayonnaise, adding the mustard, cayenne, lemon juice and cream.

FOR THE MUSTARD MAYONNAISE:
1 egg yolk, at room temperature
1 tablespoon Dijon mustard
¼ teaspoon salt
dash of cayenne pepper
½ cup (4 fl oz) light olive oil or vegetable oil
2 tablespoons fresh lemon juice
1–2 tablespoons heavy cream

1 celeriac (celery root), about 1 lb

TO MAKE THE MUSTARD MAYONNAISE, in a bowl, whisk together the egg yolk, mustard, salt and cayenne pepper until well blended. Add a little of the oil and whisk vigorously until an emulsion forms. Add a little more of the oil and whisk vigorously again to ensure the emulsion is stabilized. Then start adding the remaining oil a little at a time, beating vigorously after each addition, until it is fully absorbed. Once all of the oil has been added, the mayonnaise should be very thick. Add the lemon juice and mix well. Whisk in 1 tablespoon of the cream, and then whisk in more as needed to achieve a creamy sauce. Taste and adjust the seasonings. Set aside.

USING A SHARP KNIFE, peel the celeriac. Shred the celeriac on the medium-sized holes of a handheld shredder, with a crank-type European shredder (see page 76) or in a food processor fitted with the medium disk. To keep the celeriac from turning brown once shredded, immediately place in a bowl and add about half of the mustard mayonnaise. Mix well to coat the celeriac shreds, adding more of the mayonnaise as needed. (Cover and refrigerate any leftover mayonnaise for another use.) The celeriac should be lightly coated with the mayonnaise. Serve at once or cover and refrigerate for up to a few hours before serving. ♛

FRENCH ONION SOUP

SERVES 4

One of the most enduring memories any visitor to Paris brought home was of a steaming bowl of cheese-topped onion soup, eaten at a street stall or small cafe around the marketplace of Les Halles, especially as a postmidnight pick-me-up after a night out on the town.

1½–2 lb yellow onions, cut in half through stem end
¼ cup (2 oz) unsalted butter
1 tablespoon all-purpose flour
5 cups (40 fl oz) chicken stock, heated
1 tablespoon dark molasses
herb bouquet of 1 bay leaf, 2 fresh parsley sprigs and
  2 fresh thyme, sprigs
salt and freshly ground black pepper
pinch of cayenne pepper
2–3 tablespoons dry sherry
8–12 slices French baguette
1 cup (4 oz) shredded Gruyère cheese

LAY EACH ONION HALF on a cutting surface and cut crosswise into slices ¼ inch thick.

IN A LARGE, WIDE SAUCEPAN over medium heat, melt the butter. When hot, add the onions and sauté, stirring occasionally, until evenly golden, 20–30 minutes. Sprinkle the flour over the onions and stir until evenly distributed, 1–2 minutes. Add the stock and bring to a boil, stirring constantly. Cook until slightly thickened and smooth, about 3 minutes. Add the molasses and stir until blended. Add the herb bouquet, reduce the heat to a simmer, cover partially and simmer until the onions are tender, 30–40 minutes. Season to taste with salt and black and cayenne peppers. Remove the herb bouquet and discard. Just before serving, stir in the sherry to taste.

JUST BEFORE THE SOUP IS READY, preheat a broiler. To serve, ladle the soup into warmed deep heatproof bowls placed on a baking sheet. Carefully float 2 or 3 baguette slices on top of each bowl, then generously sprinkle the cheese on the bread slices, dividing it evenly. Place under the broiler about 4 inches from the heat and broil until the cheese melts and starts to turn golden, just a few minutes. Serve at once. 〰

"The whole of cooking can be reduced to two processes: either you want to extract the juice and the goodness out of something, whatever it is, or you want to keep them in that something. Roasting, frying, grilling, braising are all but different examples of the latter process, soup-making and boiling examples of the former one."

—X. Marcel Boulestin, French chef and cookbook author (1878–1943)

THE RETURN OF THE LEEK

In the early 1900s, leeks had nearly disappeared from menus in France, to be rediscovered by French chefs in the years after World War II. That probably explains why Americans encountered *leeks à la grecque* so often when traveling there during that time. It was hard to find leeks in the United States in the 1950s, however, unless you started your own from seed or knew a local farmer who grew them. Today, you can buy them in most well-stocked food stores and produce shops.

LEEKS A LA GRECQUE

SERVES 4

A light appetizer of leeks that have been cooked and left to cool in a fragrant mixture of stock and wine, this recipe is typical of the simple bistro dishes visitors to France in the 1950s would try to recreate when they returned home. The easy "Greek-style" treatment was also a popular way for the French to cook other vegetables such as mushrooms, artichoke hearts, celeriac or fennel. Once the leeks are combined with the onions and seasonings, simmer them very gently so they'll hold together and develop a good flavor.

2 lb young, slender leeks
1 tablespoon salt
8–10 pearl onions
¾ cup (6 fl oz) chicken stock, or as needed
⅓ cup (3 fl oz) dry white wine
3 tablespoons olive oil
1 tablespoon tomato paste
4 bay leaves
1 teaspoon peppercorns
paprika

TRIM THE LEEKS, leaving about 1 inch of the tender green tops intact and cutting them all to the same length. (Trim but do not cut off the root core.) Remove and discard any old leaves. Make a lengthwise slit along each leek to within about 2 inches of the root end. Hold each leek under cold running water and separate the leaves slightly to rinse away any dirt lodged between the layers. If the leeks are small, leave them whole; if medium-sized, cut them in half lengthwise.

USING KITCHEN STRING, tie the leeks in a bundle, securing it in 2 or 3 places. Bring a large pot half full of water to a boil over high heat. Add the salt and the leeks and boil, uncovered, for 5 minutes. Drain and let cool for a few minutes. When cool enough to handle, snip the string and separate the leeks. Set aside.

BRING A SMALL SAUCEPAN three-fourths full of water to a boil over high heat. Add the onions and boil, uncovered, for 3 minutes. Drain and plunge into cold water. When cool, trim off the root ends. Using your fingers, slip off the skins, then cut a shallow cross in the root end of each onion to keep the inner layers from protruding during cooking. Set aside.

PLACE THE LEEKS in a sauté pan or frying pan large enough to hold them in a single layer. In a small bowl, stir together the ¾ cup stock, the wine, olive oil and tomato paste until well blended and pour over the leeks. Tuck the bay leaves under the leeks, distributing them evenly in the pan, and scatter the peppercorns over the top. Arrange the onions around and among the leeks, making sure they are immersed in the liquid. The liquid should just barely cover the leeks; add more stock if needed. Place over medium heat and bring to a simmer. Reduce the heat to low and barely simmer, uncovered, until the leeks are tender and the liquid is reduced to a few spoonfuls, about 45 minutes. Remove from the heat and let cool.

TO SERVE, arrange the leeks in a single layer in a serving dish. Arrange the onions and bay leaves over the leeks, then spoon the sauce, including the peppercorns, over the top. Sprinkle with paprika and serve. ✿

"Anybody who is conscientious enough to follow simple directions can learn to cook. For example, if you are among those who have never boiled water, this is what you do: Fill a saucepan with cold water and put it on the stove. Adjust the burner to high. Let the water heat until it bubbles and surges— and that is boiling water. . . . Most cooking, even of elaborate dishes, is merely the combining of a number of very simple operations."

—James Beard, foreword to *The James Beard Cookbook* (1959)

"In *La Cuisine à Nice,* Lucien Heyraud gives a *salade niçoise* composed of young globe artichokes cut in quarters, black olives, raw pimento, quarters of tomato, and anchovy fillets. There are however as many versions of it as there are cooks in Provence, but in whatever way it is interpreted it should be a simple and rather crude country salad, with plenty of garlic, and the ingredients should be put in the bowl in large pieces, nicely arranged so that the salad looks colourful and fresh, and the dressing should be mixed in at the table."

—Elizabeth David,
Summer Cooking (1955)

SALADE NIÇOISE

SERVES 4

A signature dish of Nice, this main-course luncheon salad was another common discovery made by Americans, myself included, who visited France in the 1950s. We loved it! The traditional version is made only with raw vegetables. Gradually, though, the salad has come to include barely cooked young green beans. If you can find them, the slender, true French haricots verts are the best variety to use. You can also add wedges or slices of cooked small boiling potatoes. For the most authentic flavor, look for imported Italian or French canned tuna packed in olive oil.

½ lb young green beans
ice water, as needed
1⅛ teaspoons salt
1 lb small ripe tomatoes, cut into wedges
1 cucumber, 9–10 oz, peeled, halved lengthwise, seeded and
   cut crosswise into ¼-inch pieces
1 green bell pepper, 5–6 oz, seeded, deribbed and cut into
   ½-inch pieces
4 small green onions, including tender green tops, chopped
3–4 tablespoons coarsely chopped fresh dill
2 cans (6½ oz each) solid-pack tuna in olive oil or water,
   drained and flaked into small chunks

1 tablespoon fresh lemon juice
1 tablespoon white wine vinegar
freshly ground pepper
½ cup (4 fl oz) extra-virgin olive oil
¼ lb mesclun salad greens or other small lettuces, rinsed and well dried
4 eggs, hard cooked, peeled and quartered lengthwise
8 anchovy fillets in olive oil, rinsed and cut in half crosswise
20–24 tiny Niçoise olives or 12–16 other small black imported olives

TRIM THE BEANS and cut in half crosswise. Place in a bowl with ice water to cover. Set aside to crisp for 10–15 minutes. Bring a saucepan three-fourths full of water to a boil over high heat. Using tongs, lift the green beans from the ice water, reserving the water, and quickly plunge them into the boiling water along with 1 teaspoon of the salt. Boil until bright green but still crisp, 3–4 minutes. Using the tongs, return the beans to the ice water to cool. When cool, drain and set aside.

IN A BOWL, combine the green beans, tomatoes, cucumber, bell pepper, green onions, dill and tuna. Set aside.

IN A SMALL BOWL, combine the lemon juice, vinegar, the remaining ⅛ teaspoon salt and pepper to taste. Whisk together until the salt is dissolved. Add the olive oil and whisk again until well blended. Spoon half of the dressing over the vegetables and toss to coat evenly. Taste and adjust the seasonings.

TO SERVE, divide the salad greens among individual plates, spreading them out to form beds. Spoon the dressed vegetables onto the lettuce, dividing them equally. Place 4 egg quarters on each plate and top each quarter with half an anchovy fillet. Divide the olives evenly among the salads. Place the remaining dressing in a bowl and pass at the table.

"Any cook has his or her special prejudices, enthusiasms, and phobias and I am no exception. I am sternly against economy in cooking insofar as the quality of the ingredients is concerned. Margarine is no substitute for the best butter, nor vegetable oil for true olive oil. A salad can be ruined by poor oil and a cheap vinegar as surely as if it had been made with tired and gritty lettuce."

—Peggy Harvey,
Season to Taste (1960)

POTATO, ONION AND HAM AU GRATIN

SERVES 6

Don't let the title of this recipe fool you into thinking that it is topped with cheese. Au gratin means "with a crust," and while that crust may sometimes be formed by cheese, any French dish that forms a golden surface while baking in the oven or cooking under the broiler deserves the name. With its generous quantity of onions, this gratin is typical of the area around Lyons, in eastern France. The addition of ham transforms it into a main course, but if you leave it out, the potatoes and onions alone make an excellent side dish for roast meat or poultry.

3 tablespoons unsalted butter
2 lb yellow onions (about 5 medium), thinly sliced
5 large baking potatoes (about 3 lb), peeled and thinly sliced
salt and freshly ground pepper
freshly grated nutmeg
1 lb cooked ham, cut into slices ⅛ inch thick
1½ cups (12 fl oz) heavy cream

PREHEAT AN OVEN to 375°F. Butter a 4-quart baking dish. In a sauté pan over medium-low heat, melt the butter. When hot, add the onions and sauté until translucent, 7–10 minutes; do not allow to brown. Remove from the heat.

RINSE THE POTATO SLICES in cold water and dry thoroughly with paper towels. Place half of the potato slices in the prepared baking dish, arranging them in overlapping rows. Top with half of the sautéed onions. Season to taste with salt, pepper and nutmeg. Arrange the ham slices over the onion layer, covering it completely. Top with the remaining onions and then the potatoes, again arranging them in overlapping rows in an even layer. Pour 1¼ cups of the cream over the top, making sure that all the potato slices are moistened. Sprinkle with a little salt, pepper and nutmeg.

BAKE, basting several times with the remaining ¼ cup cream until it is used up, and then tip the dish and baste with cream from its bottom. The potatoes must always be moist on top. The gratin is ready when the potatoes have absorbed most of the cream, are very tender when pierced, and the top is golden brown, about 1½ hours. Serve directly from the dish. ☙

DEVILED CRAB

SERVES 4–6

Although it was a preparation that had been enjoyed throughout the coastal United States, especially in New Orleans, since the 19th century, deviled crab experienced a new vogue in the 1950s when crab became available to more people. Perhaps this renewed interest in a traditional dish was due to the fact that our growing knowledge of French cuisine made us more open to some of the more refined preparations of the American kitchen. In those days, the crab mixture was always baked in the crab's shell, which made for a dish that people talked about. Here, I have used a baking dish, but if you have purchased crabs from which you are extracting the meat, save the shells for cooking.

2 tablespoons unsalted butter
1 yellow onion, diced
1 small green bell pepper, seeded, deribbed and diced
1 celery stalk, diced
1½ cups (3 oz) fresh bread crumbs
⅓–½ cup (3–4 fl oz) milk
1 lb fresh-cooked crab meat, picked over to remove cartilage
  and shell fragments
2 teaspoons chopped fresh dill or 1 teaspoon dried dill
1 tablespoon fresh lemon juice
½ teaspoon salt
pinch of cayenne pepper
freshly ground black pepper

PREHEAT AN OVEN to 375°F. Butter a 1-quart baking dish.

IN A FRYING PAN over low heat, melt the butter. When hot, add the onion and sauté for 1 minute. Add the bell pepper and celery and cook, stirring frequently, for 1 2 minutes longer. Remove from the heat and set aside.

PLACE THE BREAD CRUMBS in a bowl. Stirring constantly, dribble the milk over them, adding only enough to moisten the crumbs evenly. Let stand for 5 minutes. Add the crab meat, the sautéed vegetables, dill, lemon juice, salt, and cayenne and black peppers. Mix well and spoon into the prepared baking dish.

BAKE UNTIL LIGHTLY BROWNED, 20–25 minutes. Serve immediately directly from the dish. ♛

THE VERY FIRST TIME
I ate moules marinières,
I learned a popular, amusing
way to eat them. Select
one mussel that has a good
shell and use your fork to
pull out the meat. Wipe off
the shell, then snap apart the
two halves. Use half of the
shell as your utensil for
pulling out and eating the
rest of the mussels, as well
as scooping up the liquid in
its curved bowl. Place a large
bowl at the center of the
table for discarding the other
empty shells.

MOULES MARINIERES

SERVES 4

I always visited the flea market on my trips to Paris during the winter. At lunchtime, I headed for a warm and steamy little restaurant called Chez Louisette. The chef's specialty was big bowls of mussels cooked in the traditional French way and served with crusty French bread for sopping up the broth. Make this quick dish for a weekend lunch during a month with an "r" in it, when fresh mussels are at their best.

¼ cup (2 oz) unsalted butter
¼ cup (1½ oz) minced shallot (3 large shallots)
1 small bay leaf
1 tablespoon chopped fresh thyme
1 cup (8 fl oz) dry white wine
3½–4 lb mussels, well scrubbed and debearded
6 tablespoons chopped fresh parsley
salt and freshly ground pepper

IN A LARGE POT over medium-low heat, melt the butter. When hot, add the shallot and sauté until translucent, 2–3 minutes. Add the bay leaf, thyme and wine, raise the heat to medium-high and cook until reduced slightly and the flavors are blended, about 2 minutes.

DISCARD ANY OPEN MUSSELS that do not close to the touch. Add the remaining mussels to the pot and sprinkle with 4 tablespoons of the parsley. Season to taste with salt and pepper. Cover tightly and cook, shaking the pan occasionally, until the mussels are open, about 5 minutes. Discard any mussels that did not open.

USING A SLOTTED SPOON, divide the mussels among warmed soup bowls. Spoon the broth over the mussels and sprinkle with the remaining 2 tablespoons parsley. Serve immediately. ✣

SCAMPI BACCARA

SERVES 4

1 lb medium-sized shrimp, peeled with tail fins intact
1 or 2 cloves garlic, depending upon taste and size
  of cloves, minced
2 tablespoons chopped fresh parsley
1 teaspoon chopped fresh oregano
1 tablespoon olive oil
2 tablespoons dry white wine
salt and freshly ground pepper

PREHEAT AN OVEN to 450°F. Oil a large, round, shallow baking dish, preferably 10 inches in diameter.

USING A SMALL, SHARP KNIFE, make a slit along the back of each shrimp deep enough for the shrimp to open and flatten easily; do not cut completely through. Use the tip of the knife to remove and discard the dark veinlike intestinal tract, if any. Place the shrimp in the prepared baking dish, arranging them close together in circles with the cut sides down and fanned out and the tails facing upward.

IN A SMALL BOWL, whisk together the garlic, parsley, oregano, olive oil, wine and salt and pepper to taste until well blended. Spoon evenly over the shrimp. Bake until the shrimp are pink and have curled, 8–10 minutes. Do not overbake, or they will toughen. Serve immediately directly from the baking dish. ✣

ALTHOUGH THE WORD scampi *is Italian for prawns or small lobsters, in America in the 1950s it was used to identify a dish of shrimp cooked with garlic, butter and white wine. This particular recipe, named for a once-famous restaurant in New York, replaces the butter with olive oil. Although typical of both southern French and northern Italian cooking, it is actually a good example of what, in the past decades, was called Continental cuisine.*

Zucchini Purée

Cook zucchini just a few minutes, drain and purée in a food processor fitted with the metal blade. Combine with 2 or 3 tablespoons unsalted butter, a few gratings of nutmeg and salt and pepper to taste. Heat and serve. Or substitute a little finely chopped fresh rosemary for the nutmeg.

CHICKEN BREASTS WITH TARRAGON

SERVES 4

Although tarragon had been used only sparingly in American kitchens until the 1950s, the popular French herb became the rage here in that decade, especially with chicken and fish and as a seasoning for white wine vinegar.

4 chicken breast halves, 8–9 oz each, skinned and boned (about
  6 oz each when boned)
1 tablespoon unsalted butter
1 tablespoon vegetable oil
salt and freshly ground pepper
3 tablespoons chopped shallot
1 tablespoon chopped fresh tarragon
½ cup (4 fl oz) heavy cream
fresh lemon juice, optional
chopped fresh parsley

TRIM ANY EXCESS FAT from the chicken breasts. Rinse and pat dry with paper towels. One at a time, place a chicken breast between 2 sheets of waxed paper or plastic wrap. Using a rolling pin, flatten to an even thickness of about ½ inch.

IN A LARGE SAUTÉ PAN or frying pan over medium-high heat, melt the butter with the vegetable oil. When hot, add the chicken breasts, sprinkle to taste with salt and pepper, and sauté gently, turning once, until golden, opaque throughout and the juices run clear when pierced with a knife, about 3 minutes on each side. Transfer to a warmed plate and keep warm.

POUR OFF ANY EXCESS FAT from the pan and place over medium-low heat. Add the shallot and sauté, stirring, until translucent, 1–2 minutes. Add the tarragon and cream, raise the heat to medium, and stir with a wooden spoon, scraping up any browned bits from the pan bottom and blending well. Cook, stirring, until bubbling and thickened slightly, 2–3 minutes. Season to taste with salt and pepper and a squeeze of lemon juice, if desired.

RETURN THE CHICKEN BREASTS to the pan and turn each breast several times in the sauce until well coated and hot. Transfer to a warmed serving plate or individual plates and spoon the remaining sauce over the breasts. Sprinkle with parsley and serve at once. ♛

French wine vinegars flavored with tarragon or garlic cloves gave American cooks new options in dressing salads and seasoning other dishes as well.

IN THE 1950s and early 1960s, Americans were traveling to England as well as France. Most of them would come back with memories of eating just this sort of English fare. I learned from my local butcher to use lamb kidneys, which are more tender and mild tasting than those of beef or veal, and to add them to the beef only for the last stage of cooking. This dish requires a deep, oval 1 1/2-quart pie dish with a rim. Traditional English pie dishes often come with a pastry funnel, which stands in the center of the dish and helps both to support the crust and vent the escaping steam. Serve the pie as the main course of a casual weekend meal.

STEAK AND KIDNEY PIE

SERVES 4

3 tablespoons unsalted butter
2 tablespoons vegetable oil
2 yellow onions, sliced
about ½ cup (2½ oz) all-purpose flour
1½ lb top round of beef, cut into 1½-inch cubes
½ cup (4 fl oz) dry red wine
½ cup (4 fl oz) beef stock
3 fresh thyme sprigs
3 fresh parsley sprigs
1 bay leaf
½ teaspoon salt
freshly ground pepper
1 tablespoon Worcestershire sauce
½ cup (4 fl oz) tarragon vinegar
1 cup (8 fl oz) water
6 lamb kidneys

FOR THE PASTRY:
1¾ cups (9 oz) all-purpose flour
¼ teaspoon salt
½ cup (4 oz) unsalted butter, chilled and cut into small pieces
1 egg, separated
2 tablespoons ice water
1 tablespoon fresh lemon juice
1 teaspoon cold water

IN A LARGE SAUTÉ PAN or frying pan over medium-low heat, melt 1 tablespoon of the butter with the oil. When hot, add the onions and sauté until translucent, 7–10 minutes. Remove from the heat and, using a slotted spoon, transfer the onions to a deep, heavy pot.

SPREAD OUT THE FLOUR on a plate. Coat the beef cubes evenly with the flour, shaking off any excess. Return the sauté pan or frying pan to medium-high heat and add 1 tablespoon of the remaining butter. Working in batches, add the beef cubes and sauté until lightly browned on all sides, 6–8 minutes. Transfer to the pot holding the onions.

ADD THE WINE and stock to the pan and stir with a wooden spoon over medium-high heat, scraping up any browned bits from the pan bottom and blending well. Add to the beef and onions. Gather together the thyme, parsley and bay leaf into a bouquet and tie securely with kitchen string, then add to the pot along with the salt and pepper to taste and the Worcestershire sauce. Place over low heat and bring to a simmer. Cover and simmer until the beef is tender, 1½–1¾ hours.

MEANWHILE, combine the vinegar and water in a bowl. Slice the kidneys in half lengthwise through the core and remove the membranes and the core. Add the kidneys to the vinegar mixture and let soak for 1 hour. Drain and pat dry.

WHILE THE KIDNEYS are soaking, make the pastry: Sift together the flour and salt into a bowl. Drop in the butter and, using your fingertips or a pastry blender, blend the ingredients together, working quickly, until the mixture resembles tiny peas. In a small bowl beat together the egg yolk, ice water and lemon juice. Slowly add to the flour mixture, stirring and tossing gently with a fork to form a rough mass. Gather the dough into a ball, enclose in plastic wrap and chill for 30 minutes.

PREHEAT AN OVEN to 350°F. On a floured work surface, roll out the dough into an oval or round about ⅛ inch thick and 12 inches in diameter and set aside on waxed paper.

RINSE THE SAUTÉ PAN or frying pan and place over medium-high heat. Add the remaining 1 tablespoon butter. When hot, add the kidneys and sauté quickly, turning often, until lightly browned on all sides, about 3 minutes. With a slotted spoon, remove the kidneys and set aside.

REMOVE THE HERB BOUQUET from the beef and discard. Add the kidneys to the beef and stir to mix well. Taste and adjust the seasonings. Transfer to a 1½-quart pie dish (see note opposite), then let the mixture cool for 5–10 minutes. Carefully transfer the pastry to the dish, draping it over the top. Trim as necessary to leave a 1-inch overhang, then fold the edges of the pastry under and flute attractively. With a sharp knife, cut a few slits in the pastry to allow steam to escape. In a small bowl, whisk together the egg white and cold water. Brush the pastry with the mixture.

BAKE UNTIL THE PASTRY is golden brown, 20–25 minutes. Remove from the oven and let stand for a few minutes, then cut the pastry top into wedges and serve hot. ❧

"Nobody has ever been able to find out why the English regard a glass of wine added to a soup or stew as a reckless foreign extravagance and at the same time spend pounds on bottled sauces, gravy powders, soup cubes, ketchups and artificial flavourings. If every kitchen contained a bottle each of red wine, white wine and inexpensive port for cooking, hundreds of store cupboards could be swept clean for ever of the cluttering debris of commercial sauce bottles and all synthetic aids to flavouring."

—Elizabeth David, *French Country Cooking* (1951)

"[Modern French housewives] still understand and grow and use unquestioningly the old herbs for the old dishes, and they still cook and eat in a seasonal pattern. When lamb is at its best, thyme on the hillsides will have sent out new supple shoots to tie around it for roasting, and the peas and lettuces are at their tenderest, all to make a feast provincial families wait for as patiently and instinctively as birds do the coming spring."

—M.F.K. Fisher, *The Cooking of Provincial France* (1968)

LEG OF LAMB WITH BEANS

SERVES 6–8

If one dish during this period summed up the appeal of French country cooking, this would be it. In the way it looked, smelled and tasted, it really got the gastronomic juices flowing. It certainly made a great impression on me, and everyone else I knew who traveled to Provence.

2¼ cups (1 lb) dried white beans
1 celery stalk, cut in half crosswise
1 carrot, cut in half crosswise
1 yellow onion, cut in half through the stem end, plus 2 lb
  yellow onions (about 5 medium), thinly sliced
1 bay leaf
2 tablespoons unsalted butter
2 lb baking potatoes, peeled and thinly sliced
salt and freshly ground pepper
1 leg of lamb, 6–7 lb
1 cup (8 fl oz) chicken stock, heated

SORT THROUGH THE BEANS, discarding any discolored ones or impurities. Rinse the beans and place in a bowl. Add cold water to cover generously and let stand for 3 hours. Alternatively, place the beans in a pot with water to cover over high heat and bring to a simmer. Cover the pot, remove it from the heat and let the beans soak for 1–1½ hours.

DRAIN THE BEANS, place in a (or return to the) pot and add water to cover by 3 inches. Add the celery, carrot, the halved onion and bay leaf. Bring to a boil over medium-high heat, reduce the heat to medium-low, cover and simmer until the beans are almost done but still firm, 1–1¼ hours. Using a slotted spoon, scoop out the vegetables and bay leaf and discard. Drain off the liquid from the beans.

POSITION A RACK in the lower third of an oven and preheat to 350°F.

IN A LARGE SAUTÉ PAN over medium-low heat, melt the butter. When hot, add the sliced onions and sauté until translucent, 7–10 minutes; do not allow to brown. Spread half of the onions in a 4-quart baking dish, top with half of the beans and then half of the potatoes in overlapping rows of circles, seasoning each layer lightly with salt and pepper. Repeat with the remaining onions, beans and potatoes, again seasoning lightly. Cover with aluminum foil and bake for 15 minutes.

TRIM AWAY all but a very thin layer of fat from the lamb. Remove the baking dish from the oven and carefully place a small custard cup or ramekin, bottom up, down into the middle of the bean mixture. It should be slightly lower than the level of the vegetables. Rest the meaty side of the lamb leg on it. (This prevents the lamb from sinking down onto the bottom of the dish.)

PLACE THE BAKING DISH in the oven and roast until the leg is browned and done as desired. Check for doneness by inserting an instant-read thermometer in the thickest part of the leg away from the bone. It should register 135° 140°F for pink, which will take about 1½ hours, or 150°F for medium, which will take about 1¾ hours. As the lamb roasts, baste the lamb and potatoes every 15 minutes or so with the chicken stock, and begin testing for doneness after 1 hour.

REMOVE THE BAKING DISH from the oven and transfer the leg to a cutting board. Cover loosely with aluminum foil and let rest for 10 minutes before carving, then carve and serve with the beans, onions and potatoes. ✿

"Theoretically a good cook should be able to perform under any circumstances, but cooking is much easier, pleasanter, and more efficient if you have the right tools. Good equipment which will last for years does not seem outrageously expensive when you realize that a big, enameled-iron casserole costs no more than a 6-rib roast, that a large enameled skillet can be bought for the price of a leg of lamb, and that a fine paring knife may cost less than two small lamb chops."

Simone Beck, Louisette Bertholle and Julia Child, *Mastering the Art of French Cooking* (1961)

BLANQUETTE DE VEAU

SERVES 4

Blanquette de veau is a simple white stew in which veal is first gently simmered in water with aromatic vegetables and then the mixture is enriched with egg yolks and cream. A specialty of the Languedoc region of southern France, it quickly became a favorite with Americans because it is easy to make, as well as tasty and satisfying.

2 lb veal shoulder, trimmed of fat and cut into 1½-inch cubes
12 small white boiling onions, about 1 inch in diameter, peeled
 and a shallow cross cut into each root end
2 carrots, peeled and thinly sliced
2 or 3 cloves garlic, depending upon taste and size of cloves,
 minced
2 or 3 fresh thyme sprigs
salt
6 oz small fresh mushrooms, wiped clean and thinly sliced
2 tablespoons unsalted butter
2 tablespoons all-purpose flour
3 egg yolks
1 cup (8 fl oz) heavy cream
1–2 teaspoons fresh lemon juice
white pepper
chopped fresh parsley

IN A HEAVY POT over medium-high heat, combine the veal cubes and water to cover. Bring to a boil, skimming off any foam that forms on the surface. Reduce the heat to low and add the onions, carrots, garlic, thyme and salt to taste. Cover and simmer gently until the meat is almost tender, about 1 hour.

ADD THE MUSHROOMS and continue to simmer gently until the veal is very tender, about 30 minutes longer. Keep warm.

Chicken Masquerading as Veal

If you cannot find good veal scallops, place boned chicken breasts between two sheets of plastic wrap, pound them flat, dip in beaten egg and then fine dried bread crumbs, and cook for a couple of minutes (no more) on each side in a mixture of olive oil and unsalted butter.

Garnish with lemon wedges, anchovies and capers, and serve with buttered medium or wide noodles. It isn't Wiener schnitzel, but it's very good.

IN THE TOP PAN OF A DOUBLE BOILER over (but not touching) simmering water in the bottom pan of the double boiler, melt the butter. Using a whisk or wooden spoon, stir in the flour and cook, stirring, until it bubbles, 1–2 minutes; do not let it brown. Remove from the heat and gradually pour 1½ cups of the liquid from the veal into the flour mixture, stirring constantly, until the sauce is smooth.

RETURN TO LOW HEAT and cook, stirring frequently, until thickened, 2–3 minutes. Pour water to a depth of about 1 inch in the bottom pan of the double boiler and bring to a simmer over medium-low heat. Place the top pan over (but not touching) the simmering water.

IN A BOWL, beat together the egg yolks and cream until blended. Stir the egg yolk mixture into the mixture in the double boiler, then continue to stir until thickened and creamy, 5–10 minutes; do not allow to boil. Season to taste with lemon juice, white pepper and salt.

REMOVE THE THYME SPRIGS from the veal and discard. Drain the veal and vegetables; reserve the broth for another use. Arrange the veal and vegetables on a warmed serving dish. Pour the white sauce over the top and sprinkle with parsley. Serve immediately. ♛

CARROTS VICHY

SERVES 4

In the past, the French, and American visitors to France, believed that carrots were at their best when cooked in mineral water from the area of Vichy, in the central part of the country. While simmering them in special water may have made a difference back in the days when most public drinking water was pretty foul, I think the real reason carrots Vichy caught on with Americans was because the recipe came along at a time when most of the vegetables they were used to eating were canned. Rediscovering fresh carrots, their flavor enhanced by butter, sugar, salt, lemon juice and mint—not to mention the water—must have been a revelation.

1 lb large carrots (6 or 7)
¼ cup (2 oz) unsalted butter
2 tablespoons sugar
½ teaspoon salt
1 cup water, or as needed
1 lemon
4 or 5 fresh mint sprigs

PEEL THE CARROTS, then slice thinly on the diagonal. You should have about 3 cups. Put the carrot slices into a heavy saucepan along with the butter, sugar, salt and 1 cup water. Place over medium heat and bring to a boil. Reduce the heat to medium-low and simmer gently, uncovered, until the liquid is reduced to 1–2 tablespoons syrup and the carrots are tender, 20–25 minutes. Check the carrots occasionally to be sure they are not scorching, adding a little more water and stirring as needed. Transfer to a serving dish.

USING A ZESTER or a fine-holed shredder, and holding the lemon over the carrots, shred the zest from the skin evenly over the carrots. Garnish with the mint sprigs and serve at once.

GLEN ELLEN POTATO CAKE

SERVES 4

I first tasted this crisp cake of shredded, frying pan–browned potatoes at the home of a Frenchwoman named Thérèse Bacon, who was famous in the Sonoma valley for her interpretations of classic French dishes. The recipe couldn't be simpler.

1½ lb baking potatoes
4 tablespoons (2 oz) unsalted butter
salt and freshly ground pepper

PEEL THE POTATOES and shred on the medium holes of a handheld shredder. Rinse in several changes of cold water to remove the starch, and then dry well on paper towels. (If you have a salad spinner, spin the shredded potatoes first to remove excess water, then dry on paper towels.)

IN A 12-INCH FRYING PAN over medium-low heat, melt 2 table-spoons of the butter, tipping the pan to coat the bottom evenly. When hot, add the potatoes and pack down firmly into a cake about 1 inch thick. Cook, uncovered, until golden brown on the bottom, about 15 minutes. Loosen the edges and bottom of the potato cake with a spatula, and invert a plate on top of the frying pan. Holding the plate and pan together, turn them over so the cake falls onto the plate. Lift off the frying pan and return it to the burner. Add the remaining 2 tablespoons butter to the pan and allow it to melt over medium-low heat. Slide the potato cake back into the pan, browned side up. Cook the second side until crisp and golden brown and the cake is cooked through, about 15 minutes.

AGAIN, loosen the cake from the pan and slide it out onto a warmed serving plate. Season to taste with salt and pepper. Serve at once, cut into wedges. ⚜

"Summer cooking implies a sense of immediacy, a capacity to capture the essence of the fleeing moment."
—Elizabeth David

ON MY FIRST TRIP to France, I remember noticing in the markets that all the beets for sale had already been cooked whole. This made me curious and I asked around. I was told that during the day, when country bakery ovens were not in use, bakers would slide in big trays of beets to bake from the heat retained in the brick walls. The baking concentrated and caramelized the vegetable's natural sugars, resulting in a flavor remarkably better than that of the watery boiled beets Americans ate at the time— and, to my astonishment, still eat. If you are one of the many who do not like beets, try baking them and you will change your mind.

BAKED BEETS

SERVES 4–6

4–6 medium beets
2 tablespoons unsalted butter
salt and freshly ground pepper

PREHEAT AN OVEN to 450°F.

CUT OFF THE TOPS from the beets, leaving about ½ inch of the stem intact. Do not trim off the root end, or the beets will "bleed" while cooking. Put the beets in the center of a large sheet of aluminum foil. Bring together the sides and fold to form a secure package, making 1 or 2 slits in the top to allow steam to escape. Place the package on a baking sheet. Bake the beets until tender, 45–75 minutes; the timing will depend upon the size of the beets. To test for doneness, open a corner of the package and pierce a beet with the tip of a knife. Remove from the oven, open the package and let cool slightly. Trim the stem and root ends, strip the peel from the beets with your fingers and slice them.

IN A SAUTÉ PAN or frying pan over medium heat, melt the butter. When hot, add the beets and heat through, turning as necessary. Season to taste with salt and pepper and serve at once. ☙

BAKED BICYCLE CORN

SERVES 4

Gordon Tevis, who was a member of an old California family and lived in the Sonoma hills in a beautiful country home known as the de Bretteville house, of the Spreckels sugar family, was a big fan of bicycle corn. He loved to entertain, and with this corn pudding as a first course, he started a local trend of slitting the fresh corn kernels and scraping them off the cob. Sometimes he'd add minced fresh chives or green onion to the mixture.

Only just-picked corn will thicken up properly during baking. I recommend that you seek out a good local source—a roadside stand, a produce shop, a high-quality market. Check the silks beneath the husks. If they look translucent and still slightly green, you can use the corn for this recipe. If the silks have turned brown, forget it.

4 or 5 ears of corn, husks and silks removed
⅓ cup (3 fl oz) heavy cream
salt and freshly ground pepper
freshly grated nutmeg

PREHEAT AN OVEN to 375°F. Butter a shallow 1-quart baking dish.

WIPE THE EARS OF CORN CLEAN with a paper towel. Working with 1 ear of corn at a time, rest the ear at an angle, stem end down, in a wide shallow pan. Using a very sharp paring knife and holding the ear firmly, make a cut lengthwise down the middle of each row of kernels. Holding the ear at a higher angle and using the blunt edge of the knife blade held perpendicular to the corn, carefully scrape all the pulp out of the kernels into the pan. There should be about 2 cups. Stir in the cream and season to taste with salt, pepper and nutmeg. Blend well. Transfer the mixture to the prepared baking dish.

BAKE UNTIL THE CORN THICKENS and puffs up slightly and is lightly browned across the surface, 30–35 minutes. Serve immediately directly from the dish. ♕

DURING THE 1950s, when I lived in Sonoma, a local farming family had a cornfield right on the edge of town, near the high school. They grew the then-popular Golden Bantam corn. Starting in August and on into the fall, you could drive up to their farmhouse, honk your horn and tell either one of the sons exactly how many ears of corn you wanted, what size and what age. He would then hop onto a bicycle and pedal out into the field to pick whatever corn you asked for, then pedal back and put it in a bag. You'd pay for it, rush home and cook and eat it immediately. Time was of the essence because the sugars in corn begin changing to starch within seven minutes of picking. That fresh-picked corn was the sweetest corn you can possibly imagine.

Omelet Variations

The list of possible omelet fillings is virtually endless. Here are a few suggestions:

* Add a pinch of herbes de Provence (see page 108) to the egg mixture before cooking.

* Lightly fill with fresh tomato salsa.

* Layer 6–8 fresh, tender spinach leaves and 1 tablespoon crumbled feta or shredded Monterey Jack cheese down the center just before folding.

* Fill with sautéed mushroom slices and diced green onions.

* Fill with grated tart apples and sharp Cheddar or crumbled blue cheese.

* Fill with julienned thinly sliced ham and sautéed red pepper strips.

* Add your own favorite cheese or chopped fresh herb.

A pan 8 inches in diameter is the perfect size for a three-egg omelet, and you can't do better than the heavy, nonstick omelet pans available today.

CHUCK'S FAVORITE OMELET

SERVES 1

Making an omelet seems to be a rite of passage for anyone interested in French cooking. My advice is to use a good omelet pan with shallow, sloping sides that will allow you to fold and slide out the eggs easily. My other piece of advice is to take your time. With a little practice, you'll get the technique down for folding the omelet, and even your mistakes will taste good. You'll also learn how you like your omelet cooked, with the center solid or runny, by which I mean soft and creamy rather than uncooked. I like my omelets runny and absolutely plain, although you can add any one of the suggested fillings (see left).

3 eggs
1 or 2 pinches of salt
1 tablespoon water
freshly ground pepper
1 teaspoon unsalted butter

IN A BOWL, combine the eggs, salt, water and pepper to taste. Lightly beat with a fork until blended. Place an 8-inch omelet pan over medium-high heat and heat until a drop of water flicked onto the hot surface of the pan dances. When the pan is ready, quickly swirl the butter around until it melts and foams. When the foaming subsides, pour in the eggs, shaking the pan at the same time to keep the eggs moving over the heat. Reduce the heat to medium, then quickly and lightly stir the eggs with a plastic or wooden spatula, or continue to shake the pan until the desired consistency is reached: a creamy center is usually preferred.

AT THIS POINT, add any desired filling across the center of the omelet at a right angle to the handle of the pan. With the handle of the pan in one hand and the spatula in the other, start rolling the omelet from the handle side, tipping the pan forward so that about one-fourth of the omelet rolls onto itself. Then reverse your grip on the handle so that your hand is on the underside, and invert the pan over a plate. This motion will slide and roll the omelet onto the plate with the folded portion underneath, leaving a smooth surface on top. Serve immediately. ♛

FRENCH SOFT SCRAMBLED EGGS

SERVES 2 OR 3

6 eggs
salt and freshly ground pepper
½ cup (4 oz) unsalted butter
3 tablespoons heavy cream, optional

IN A BOWL, combine the eggs with salt and pepper to taste. Beat with a whisk or fork until well blended.

SET A HEATPROOF BOWL or the top pan of a double boiler over (but not touching) simmering water in a saucepan or the bottom pan of the double boiler. Melt ¼ cup of the butter in the bowl or top pan. Add the beaten eggs and stir slowly and continuously with a whisk until the eggs begin to thicken. Keep stirring and scraping the sides and bottom of the pan to ensure that the eggs thicken evenly and become creamy without lumps. This is a leisurely process, so allow about 20 minutes.

WHEN THE EGGS ARE CREAMY, cut the remaining ¼ cup butter into small cubes and add to the eggs along with the cream, if using. Stir briefly until the butter melts and is fully incorporated. Serve immediately or keep warm over hot (not simmering) water for up to 30 minutes. ♛

Tomatoes Filled with Scrambled Eggs

Cut off the top one-fourth to one-third of small tomatoes or large plum tomatoes. Scoop out the seeds and center pulp, leaving sturdy sides. Stand the tomatoes upright in a baking dish, brush the insides with melted unsalted butter and bake in a preheated 350°F oven until the pulp is cooked slightly but still firm, about 5 minutes. Fill immediately with soft scrambled eggs that have been seasoned with salt, pepper and a little chopped green onion. Serve immediately.

QUICHE LORRAINE

SERVES 6–8

The northeastern French province of Lorraine gave us this traditional savory tart of eggs, bacon and cheese that seemed to be on every weekend brunch table and ladies' luncheon menu by the mid-1960s. Given here are the classic filling ingredients. Some versions add chopped onion or leek that has been sautéed in butter, a nod to the cooking traditions of neighboring Alsace.

FOR THE PASTRY:
1¼ cups (6½ oz) all-purpose flour
½ teaspoon salt
½ cup (4 oz) unsalted butter, chilled and cut into small cubes
1–2 tablespoons ice water

FOR THE FILLING:
6 slices lean bacon
¾ cup (6 fl oz) heavy cream, at room temperature
¾ cup (6 fl oz) milk, at room temperature
3 eggs, at room temperature
1 tablespoon unsalted butter, melted
1 cup (4 oz) shredded Gruyère cheese
salt and freshly ground black pepper
cayenne pepper
freshly grated nutmeg

TO MAKE THE PASTRY, in a bowl, stir together the flour and salt. Drop in the butter and, using a pastry blender or your fingertips, work the ingredients together quickly until crumbly and the mixture resembles oatmeal. Then, while quickly stirring and tossing with a fork, add the ice water a little at a time just until the dough begins to hold together. Gather into a ball, wrap in plastic wrap and refrigerate for 30 minutes.

POSITION A RACK in the lower third of an oven and preheat to 425°F. On a lightly floured work surface, using your hands, flatten the ball of dough into a round cake. Dust it with flour and then roll out into a round 11 inches in diameter. Fit carefully into a 9- or 10-inch tart pan, or a 9-inch glass pie dish. If using a tart pan, trim the dough even with the pan rim. If using a pie dish, trim the dough to allow a 1-inch overhang, then fold under the overhang and flute the edges. Prick the dough in several places with fork tines and chill for 10 minutes.

PARTIALLY BAKE THE PASTRY SHELL until it just begins to color, 10–12 minutes. If the pastry puffs up during baking, prick again with a fork to release the steam. Remove from the oven and set aside. Reduce the oven temperature to 375°F.

TO MAKE THE FILLING, in a frying pan over medium-high heat, fry the bacon until crisp and golden, 3–5 minutes. Transfer to paper towels to drain. When cool enough to handle, crumble into small bits. Scatter the crumbled bacon over the bottom of the pastry shell.

IN A BOWL, combine the cream, milk, eggs and melted butter. Using a whisk or fork, beat until well blended. Stir in the cheese and season to taste with salt and black and cayenne peppers. Pour into the prepared pastry shell and sprinkle the top lightly with nutmeg.

BAKE UNTIL THE CUSTARD IS SET and the tip of a knife stuck into the center of the custard comes out clean, 25–30 minutes. Remove from the oven and let stand for several minutes before serving. ♛

A SECRET FOR PERFECT SOUFFLÉS

You'll get the highest-rising soufflé if you start with the egg whites at room temperature and beat them in an unlined copper bowl with a balloon whisk. Through a harmless chemical reaction, the whites adhere to the copper, allowing more air to be beaten into them and yielding up to one-third more volume. To check if the beaten whites are at "soft peak" stage, lift the whisk straight out of the bowl and invert it. The whites adhering to the whisk should form peaks that stay upright but bend slightly at the tip.

Making a Soufflé Collar

Cut a strip of parchment paper or aluminum foil 7 inches wide and about 3 inches longer than the circumference of the dish. Fold it in half lengthwise and set it around the exterior of the dish, overlapping at the ends and with the top of the paper extended 2–3 inches above the rim of the dish. Secure with ovenproof kitchen string or a straight pin.

CHEESE SOUFFLE

SERVES 4

Beautifully showy and seeming to defy gravity, the soufflé understandably became the icon of French cooking for Americans in the late 1950s and the 1960s.

2 tablespoons unsalted butter
2 tablespoons all-purpose flour
1 cup (8 fl oz) milk, heated
4 egg yolks
½ cup (2 oz) shredded Gruyère cheese
½ cup (2 oz) freshly grated Parmesan cheese
salt and freshly ground black pepper
cayenne pepper
1 tablespoon Madeira wine
5 egg whites, at room temperature

PREHEAT AN OVEN to 350°F. Select a 1½-quart soufflé dish. Make a collar for the dish (see left). Do not grease the collar or the dish.

IN A SAUCEPAN over medium-low heat, melt the butter. When hot, add the flour and whisk until blended. Cook, stirring vigorously, for 2 minutes; do not allow to brown. Gradually pour the milk into the flour mixture, whisking constantly until smooth. Raise the heat to medium and continue to cook, stirring constantly, until the sauce is smooth, thick and comes to a boil, 2–3 minutes. Cook for a few seconds longer, then remove from the heat and let cool for 5 minutes. In a bowl, whisk the egg yolks until pale yellow, 1–2 minutes. Add a little of the hot sauce to the yolks and beat until blended. Gradually stir the yolks into the sauce. Add the Gruyère and Parmesan cheeses, salt and black and cayenne peppers to taste, and the Madeira. Stir to mix well. Set aside.

IN A CLEAN, DRY BOWL, and using a clean whisk or an electric mixer, beat the egg whites until soft peaks form. Spoon about one-fourth of the egg whites into the sauce and, using a rubber spatula, stir gently to blend and lighten the mixture. Gently fold in the remaining egg whites just until no white streaks remain. Spoon the mixture into the prepared soufflé dish. Bake until puffed and lightly browned, 35–40 minutes. Serve immediately on warmed plates. ✾

ROUND COUNTRY LOAF

MAKES I LOAF

Travels in Europe introduced many Americans raised on packaged loaves to wonderful fresh-from-the-oven bread. This recipe results in a good approxi mation of the kind of rustic country loaf you still find in France or Italy.

1 package (2½ teaspoons) active dry yeast
1 teaspoon sugar
2 cups lukewarm water (110°F)
5 cups (1½ lb) unbleached all-purpose flour
1 tablespoon salt
cornmeal

IN A SMALL BOWL, dissolve the yeast and sugar in ¼ cup of the water and let stand until foamy, about 3 minutes.

IN A LARGE BOWL, using a wooden spoon, mix together the flour and salt. Stir in the remaining 1¾ cups water and the yeast mixture to form a soft dough that holds its shape. Turn out the dough onto a floured work surface and knead by hand until smooth, elastic and not sticky, about 10 minutes, adding a little flour if needed.

WARM A BOWL WITH HOT WATER, dry with a kitchen towel and coat the inside with butter. Shape the dough into a ball, place in the prepared bowl, cover with buttered plastic wrap and let rise in a warm place until doubled in bulk, 1–1½ hours.

SPRINKLE A BAKING PAN with cornmeal. Turn out the dough onto the floured work surface, punch down and knead a few times to dispel any air pockets. Shape into a ball, roll lightly in flour and place on the prepared baking pan. The dough should remain in a sphere; if it doesn't, knead in a little flour. Cover loosely with a kitchen towel and let rise in a warm place until doubled in bulk, 30–40 minutes. Meanwhile, preheat an oven to 425°F.

USING A VERY SHARP KNIFE, make a ½-inch-deep slash in the top of the loaf. Place the baking pan in the oven and bake for 15 minutes. Reduce the oven temperature to 375°F and bake until the loaf is crusty, golden brown and sounds hollow when tapped on the under-side, 30–40 minutes longer. Transfer to a wire rack to cool. ♔

SIMULATING A BRICK OVEN

Your bread will rise better and develop a thin, crisp crust if you simulate the dry, radiant heat of a brick baker's oven inside your home oven. One way to do this is to buy a covered earthenware bread baker (called a clay cloche), which holds the loaf while it bakes. You could also, as I was taught to do by Elizabeth David, place the loaf on a heavy baking sheet and invert a large oven-proof earthenware mixing bowl over it. Another alternative is to line the bottom of a gas oven, or the bottom shelf of an electric oven, with ceramic baking tiles and place the pan directly on them.

POT DE CREME POTS

For the most charming and authentic presentation of this dessert, look for French pot de crème pots. Made of white porcelain, these small cups have rounded sides with little handles. They come with matching lids that prevent skins from forming on the surface of the custards during baking. If you can't find the pots, custard cups or porcelain ramekins will do fine, with small sheets of aluminum foil substituted for the lids.

PETITS POTS DE CREME AU CHOCOLAT

SERVES 6

Before our present obsession with chocolate mousse, lovers of French cooking were filling individual porcelain pots with intensely rich, dense chocolate custard. Although this marvelous dessert looks very sophisticated, there is no great secret to success. Just start with the right kind of small, heatproof cups and a good-quality French, Swiss or Belgian bittersweet chocolate such as Callebaut, Valrhona, Tobler or Lindt. Mix the ingredients following the recipe instructions precisely, then strain the mixture to rid it of any lumps. Baking the filled pots in a water bath provides the gentle, moist heat the custard needs to thicken properly.

1 cup (8 fl oz) heavy cream
2 oz bittersweet chocolate, chopped into small pieces
3 egg yolks
2 tablespoons sugar
1–2 teaspoons vanilla extract
boiling water, as needed

PREHEAT AN OVEN to 325°F.

POUR THE CREAM into a saucepan over medium heat and heat until small bubbles appear around the edges of the pan. Remove from the heat and stir in the chocolate until melted and well blended. Let cool slightly.

IN A BOWL, combine the egg yolks and sugar. Using a whisk, beat until pale yellow and thick enough to fall from the whisk in a lazy ribbon, about 5 minutes. Slowly stir in the warm chocolate cream and add the vanilla extract to taste.

PLACE SIX ¼-CUP POT DE CREME POTS with lids or ramekins in a baking pan. Pour the chocolate mixture through a fine-mesh sieve into the pots or ramekins, dividing it evenly. Pour boiling water into the baking pan to a depth of 1 inch. Cover the pots with their lids or the ramekins with a single sheet of aluminum foil. Bake until the custards are just set at the edges, 15–20 minutes. They should still tremble slightly.

REMOVE THE BAKING PAN from the oven. Place the pots or ramekins on a wire rack, remove the lids or aluminum foil and let cool at room temperature. When cool, cover again and refrigerate for at least 4 hours, or for up to 2 days, before serving. ✿

Fruit Compote with Cassis

Those who traveled to France in the 1950s learned how easily the black currant syrup known as cassis could transform ordinary fruit salad into a special dessert.

Combine balls of cantaloupe, honeydew or papaya with raspberries or strawberries or any other combination of cut-up fruit. Combine the juice of 2 or 3 oranges, the juice of ½ lemon and 3–4 tablespoons cassis syrup. Sweeten to taste with honey or sugar. Pour over the fruits and chill, turning the fruits over in the juice several times.

Chocolate Madeleines

*Beat together 2 egg yolks,
¹/₂ cup (4 oz) sugar and ¹/₂ cup
(1¹/₂ oz) Dutch-process
cocoa. Fold in ¹/₂ cup (2 oz)
sifted cake flour, 1 teaspoon
baking powder and a pinch of
salt. Then beat in ¹/₂ cup (4 oz)
unsalted butter, softened, and
2 teaspoons rum flavoring.
Whisk 2 egg whites until stiff
and fold in. Brush madeleine
molds with melted butter and
fill each shell two-thirds full.
Bake in a 425°F oven until
risen and firm, 10–15 minutes.
Makes 22–24.*

MADELEINES

MAKES 12 MADELEINES

These little sponge cakes, immortalized by Marcel Proust in Remembrance
of Things Past, *are at their most memorable when eaten as Proust himself liked them, fresh from the oven, still warm and a little crisp on the
outside. As madeleines tend to dry out quickly, home-baked ones are best.
Madeleine pans (see opposite) were among the first baking pans that I
brought into America in the late 1950s, and they were the most popular
items for a year or two in the store. If you use a black nonstick madeleine
pan, decrease the oven temperature by 25°F or shorten the baking time
by a few minutes. You can find orange-flower water imported from France
in specialty-food shops.*

½ cup (2 oz) cake flour
½ teaspoon baking powder
1 egg
¼ cup (2 oz) granulated sugar
2 teaspoons orange-flower water
¼ cup (2 oz) unsalted butter, softened
confectioners' sugar

POSITION A RACK in the lower third of an oven and preheat to 400°F. Generously butter the molds of a 12-place madeleine plaque.

SIFT TOGETHER the flour and baking powder into a bowl and set aside. In another bowl, using an electric mixer set on medium speed, beat together the egg, granulated sugar and orange-flower water for 30 seconds. Increase the speed to high and beat until the mixture has quadrupled in bulk and is very thick, about 10 minutes. Using a rubber spatula, carefully fold in the flour mixture and then the softened butter. Spoon the batter into the prepared molds, filling each one about three-fourths full.

BAKE UNTIL LIGHT BROWN around the edges and on the bottom, 10–12 minutes. Remove from the oven and then immediately remove the madeleines from the pan to a wire rack. Using a fine-mesh sieve or a sifter, dust with confectioners' sugar. Serve warm.

Made of tinned steel or aluminum, madeleine plaques traditionally have 12 shallow, shell-shaped depressions each 3 inches long that give madeleines their characteristic shape. You can sometimes find madeleinette plaques that have smaller depressions for making cakes 1½ inches long.

IN THE SAN FRANCISCO area before and after World War II, the cake to serve for any birthday party or other special occasion was caramel crunch cake, a creation from the city's now-gone Blum's pastry shop on the corner of Polk and California streets. My mother made it to great applause in Sonoma in the early 1950s. When I first ran this recipe in the Williams-Sonoma catalog in the 1970s, we received nostalgic letters from around the country.

CARAMEL CRUNCH CAKE

MAKES ONE 10-INCH CAKE; SERVES 8–10

FOR THE CAKE:
1¼ cups (5 oz) cake flour, sifted
1½ cups (12 oz) granulated sugar
6 egg yolks (½ cup)
¼ cup water
1 tablespoon fresh lemon juice
1 teaspoon vanilla extract
7 or 8 egg whites (1 cup)
1 teaspoon cream of tartar
1 teaspoon salt

FOR THE TOPPING:
1½ cups (12 oz) granulated sugar
¼ cup brewed coffee
¼ cup light corn syrup
1 tablespoon baking soda, sifted

2 cups (16 fl oz) heavy cream
2 tablespoons confectioners' sugar
2 teaspoons vanilla extract

PREHEAT AN OVEN to 375°F.

TO MAKE THE CAKE, in a bowl, stir together the flour and ¾ cup of the granulated sugar. Add the egg yolks, water, lemon juice and vanilla and, using a wooden spoon or an electric mixer set on medium speed, beat until a smooth batter forms. In another large bowl, combine the egg whites, cream of tartar and salt. Using clean beaters, beat on medium speed until a fine foam forms throughout. Gradually add the remaining ¾ cup granulated sugar and continue to beat on high speed until stiff peaks form. Pour the batter gently over the egg whites and, using a rubber spatula, fold in the batter just until blended and no white streaks remain; do not overmix. Gently spoon the batter into an ungreased 10-inch angel food cake pan or similar tube pan. Using a knife, cut through the batter several times to break up any bubbles and level the mixture.

BAKE UNTIL THE TOP SPRINGS BACK when touched, 50–55 minutes. Remove from the oven and immediately invert the pan. Rest it on the tube if it is higher than the sides of the pan, on legs if your pan has them or slide the tube over the neck of a bottle. Let the cake hang until cool, then loosen with a metal spatula and transfer to a plate.

TO MAKE THE TOPPING, in a heavy, deep saucepan, bring the granulated sugar, coffee and syrup to a boil over high heat, stirring to dissolve the sugar. Cook to the hard-crack stage (300°F) on a candy thermometer. Remove from the heat and immediately add the baking soda. Stir vigorously just until the topping thickens and pulls away from the sides of the pan (do not destroy the foam). Pour quickly into an ungreased, shallow 9-by-13-inch metal pan. Do not stir or spread. Let cool completely without moving. Knock out of the pan onto a sheet of waxed paper. Top with a second sheet and crush into coarse crumbs with a rolling pin. Cover and set aside.

USING A SERRATED KNIFE, cut the cake into 4 layers. In a bowl, combine the cream, confectioners' sugar and vanilla. Using a whisk or an electric mixer, beat until stiff. Using half of the whipped cream, spread each cake layer with cream, stacking them one on top of another. Then spread the remaining cream on the top and sides of the cake. If desired, cover and refrigerate for up to 2 hours before serving. Just before serving, generously cover the top and sides of the cake with the crushed caramel. ✺

Brandy Velvet

Like a grown-up milkshake, this popular recipe from the 1950s turns coffee ice cream into an elegant dessert.

For each serving, combine 2 tablespoons each brandy, cold strong coffee and chocolate syrup and 2 scoops coffee ice cream in a milkshake mixer. Mix at low speed until just blended. Or beat with an electric rotary beater. Serve in a wineglass.

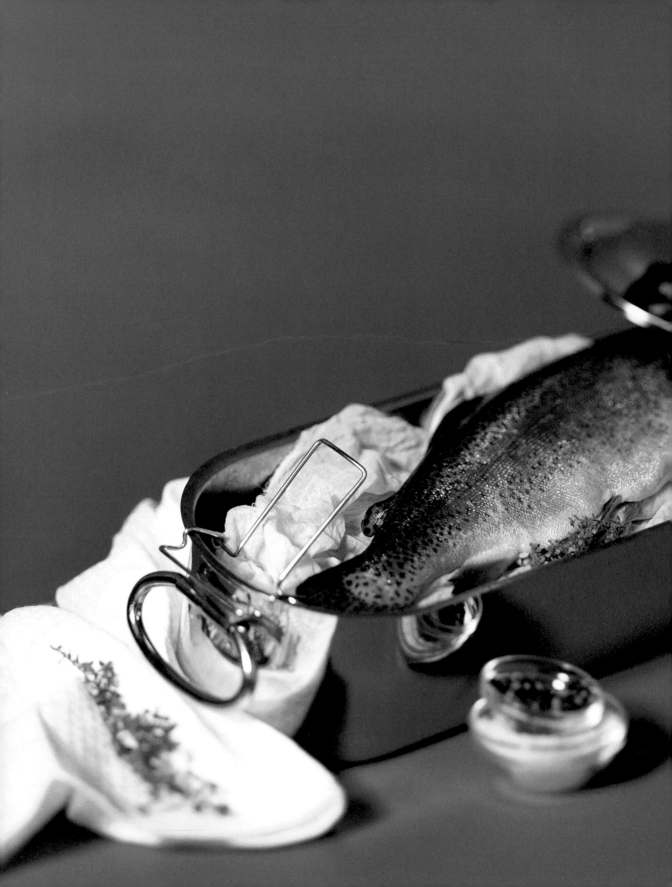

1966–1976
THE SPIRIT OF ADVENTURE

From my perspective at Williams-Sonoma, the late 1960s and early 1970s were a time when people's interest in French cooking and cooking in general both grew and deepened. Thanks to the television popularity of Julia Child and the introduction of Graham Kerr's *The Galloping Gourmet,* and spurred on by the free spirit of the hippie movement in the late 1960s, people who loved to cook became increasingly adventurous.

They were no longer satisfied with simple bistro fare alone. Exposed to French cooking through their television journeys and vacations in the French countryside, avid cooks wanted to poach whole salmon, prepare country pâtés and make showy desserts like *tarte Tatin*.

The growing awareness of the pleasures people found in good cooking was reflected in an explosion of cookbook publishing. In 1960, fewer than 100 cookbooks were published in the United States; in 1969 alone, more than 1,200 new cookbooks fought for the attention of food lovers, many of whom had begun to collect them avidly.

One excellent example of how collectible cookbooks were becoming was Time-Life Books' Foods of the World series, launched in 1968. In volume after volume, serious writers, cooking experts and photojournalists explored the cuisines of different countries and regions. Practically everyone I knew signed up to receive them through the mail. Perhaps the most attention was paid to *The Cooking of Provincial France,* authored by the legendary Sonoma-based food writer M.F.K. Fisher in consultation with New York–based cooking teacher Michael Field and Julia Child.

In response to our hunger for French food, more and more English language editions of cookbooks by the classic French chefs also began to appear, including Henri Paul Pellaprat's *The Great Book of French Cuisine* (1966), Raymond Oliver's *La Cuisine* (1969) and X. Marcel Boulestin's *Recipes of Boulestin* (1971). Simone Beck, Julia's former partner and coauthor, also gave us her *Simca's Cuisine* in 1972.

One of the foremost reasons for our growing understanding of French food, however, came from an American. Richard Olney, who was born and raised in Iowa but moved to France as a young man, brought out two now-classic books in the early 1970s: *The French Menu Cookbook* (1970) and *Simple French Food* (1974). He wrote about the food and wines of France with an accuracy and intelligence that the French both respected and embraced, and with an insight and clarity that Americans could understand. We loved having him stop by Williams-Sonoma when he was in this country promoting his books.

Even as we were all learning about French cooking, that cuisine itself was changing. The early 1970s saw chefs like Paul Bocuse and Michel Guérard lead a revolution away from classic French cuisine toward greater simplicity, lightness and freshness. In October 1973, French critics Henri Gault and Christian Millau in their *Gault-Millau* magazine christened this movement *nouvelle cuisine.*

A similar shift was also going on at home. In 1971, Alice Waters, with a group of young

The growing awareness of the pleasures people found in good cooking was reflected in an explosion of cookbook publishing.

people aspiring to be chefs, opened Chez Panisse in Berkeley. Her unique interpretations of French cooking, coupled with her reliance on fresh ingredients, made her the pioneer of what some people called New American cooking or California cuisine. That restaurant, still thriving today, was the training ground for many other great American chefs, including Jeremiah Tower and Mark Miller.

Together, *nouvelle cuisine* and its New American counterpart excited people even more about exploring the pleasures of cooking. They visited Williams-Sonoma or thumbed through our catalog in search of the best cookware to get themselves started, or the latest vinegar or oil from France to cook with.

The adventure of cooking began to lead people in other directions, too. You can see our interests expanding not only in Foods of the World, but also in such books as *Couscous and Other Good Food from Morocco* (1973) by Paula Wolfert, and *Florence Lin's Chinese Regional Cookbook* (1975), which taught us more about a cuisine that was a subject of great

interest among New York and Bay Area cooks. Jim Beard also continued to remind us how good homegrown classics could be in *James Beard's American Cookery* (1972). Most importantly, 1973 saw the publication of Marcella Hazan's *The Classic Italian Cook Book,* which played an instrumental role in the huge growth of interest in Italian cooking during the next ten years.

All these influences led *Time* magazine to proclaim the 1970s "the decade of the home cook." Considering the way Williams-Sonoma was growing, I had to agree. We opened in Beverly Hills in 1973, in Palo Alto the year after that and in Costa Mesa a year later. Our catalog, which we began in 1971 with the creative help of my good friend Jackie Mallorca, continued to grow. Recipes were developed for the catalog that reflected the trends that were happening in the world of cooking. It was an exciting period.

Kir

This classic French aperitif was very much in vogue in France by the mid-1970s. Its name honors a country priest, Père Kir, who was a great patriot during World War II and later the mayor of Dijon. A devotee of this refreshment, he urged university students to adopt it to cut down on their drunkenness.

Mix 5 parts dry white wine to 1 part cassis (black currant) syrup. Use chilled wine or serve over ice. You can also make a nonalcoholic Kir with sparkling mineral water or soda water.

PATE MAISON

SERVES 4–6

My interest in French country-style pâté recipes started around 1966, when I saw a brown-and-cream–glazed earthenware terrine that Elizabeth David had made for her shop in London. Elizabeth, whose recipes were much less rich and time-consuming than others found in most cookbooks of the time, gave me a recipe to go with it. This one is, in fact, just a well-seasoned, finely textured meat loaf meant to be eaten cold. Once cooked, it will keep, well covered, for 4 to 5 days in the refrigerator.

½ lb veal, chicken or turkey, cut into 1-inch pieces
½ lb bacon, cut into 1-inch pieces
1 clove garlic, cut in half
1 shallot, cut in half
¼ lb smoked ham, cut into 1-inch pieces
salt
freshly ground pepper
1 egg
tiny pinch of ground cinnamon
1 tablespoon Cognac or other good-quality brandy
1 bay leaf

PREHEAT AN OVEN to 400°F. In a food processor fitted with the metal blade, combine the veal or poultry, bacon, garlic and shallot and process until minced. Add the ham, salt and pepper to taste, egg, cinnamon and brandy and process until the ham is finely chopped.

TRANSFER TO A RECTANGULAR TERRINE or loaf pan with a 2-cup capacity, packing it in firmly. Smooth the top with a rubber spatula and press the bay leaf gently into the meat mixture. Bake, uncovered, until the pâté has pulled away from the sides of the dish and the top is nicely browned, about 45 minutes.

REMOVE FROM THE OVEN, let cool, cover and refrigerate for 1 day to allow the flavors to develop. Cut into slices to serve. ☙

GREEN SALAD WITH TARRAGON VINAIGRETTE

SERVES 6

I first tasted tarragon vinegar in Paris in the early 1970s. It was made by Raoul Gey and was absolutely delicious, with the bright clean taste of Champagne vinegar, made from only the tiny grapes grown in the region of the same name. The vinegar had a heady herbal aroma from the fresh tarragon sprigs slipped right into the bottle. I brought some home so that I could experiment with it. Within months we were selling tarragon vinegar, and our customers loved it. This light salad is one of the best ways I found to show off the vinegar's qualities.

2 small heads romaine lettuce
1 small English cucumber, peeled and thinly sliced
2 tablespoons tarragon vinegar
salt and freshly ground pepper
½ cup (4 fl oz) mild extra-virgin olive oil

DISCARD ANY TOUGH OR DISCOLORED OUTER LEAVES from the lettuce heads. Separate, rinse and thoroughly dry the remaining leaves, then tear into bite-sized pieces. Place in a salad bowl.

SCATTER THE CUCUMBER SLICES over the top. In a small bowl, whisk together the vinegar and salt to taste. Slowly whisk in the olive oil. Season to taste with pepper. Drizzle over the lettuce and cucumber and toss well. Serve at once. ☙

THE LEGEND OF GARLIC VINEGAR

After tarragon vinegar, the next flavored vinegar to gain a following in the United States was garlic vinegar, about which I learned an interesting legend. In France, garlic vinegar is known as *vinaigre des quatre voleurs*, "four thieves vinegar." During a plague in Marseilles in 1721, so the story goes, four thieves were released from jail to bury the victims, since no one else could be found to do so. The thieves did not succumb to the fatal disease and, in exchange for amnesty, revealed their secret: every day they drank wine in which lots of garlic had been steeped. Since then, vinegar has replaced the wine, but each bottle always contains four cloves of garlic threaded onto a skewer, in memory of the four thieves.

COQUILLES A LA NAGE

SERVES 4

Before coquilles St. Jacques, *with its topping of piped mashed potatoes, caught on in the late 1960s, those of us who loved French cooking were making this uncomplicated first course. Barely poached, and then quickly gratinéed in the oven, the scallops come out perfectly cooked.*

1 carrot, peeled and thinly sliced
1 tablespoon chopped shallot or green onion, white part only
¾ cup water
salt
¾ cup (6 fl oz) dry white wine
4 to 6 fresh mushrooms (2 oz), wiped clean and thinly sliced
1 lb bay scallops, cut into pieces if large
1 tablespoon unsalted butter
1 tablespoon all-purpose flour
½ cup (4 fl oz) heavy cream
chopped fresh parsley

PREHEAT AN OVEN to 400°F. Butter 4 scallop shells or individual gratin dishes.

IN A SAUCEPAN over medium heat, combine the carrot, shallot or green onion, water and salt to taste. Bring to a simmer, cover and cook for 10 minutes. Add the wine and return to a simmer. Add the mushrooms and cook for 2 minutes. Add the scallops and cook until just opaque throughout, 1–2 minutes longer. Drain the vegetables and scallops, reserving the liquid, then set the scallops and vegetables aside. Return the liquid to the saucepan and place over high heat. Bring to a boil and boil until reduced by half. Remove from the heat and set aside.

IN ANOTHER SAUCEPAN over low heat, melt the butter. Using a whisk or wooden spoon, stir in the flour and cook, stirring, until it bubbles, about 30 seconds; do not allow to brown. Gradually add the reduced liquid and cream, stirring constantly until the sauce is smooth. Then stir over low heat until thickened, about 3 minutes.

ARRANGE THE SCALLOPS and vegetables in the prepared shells or gratin dishes. Pour the sauce evenly over the top. Bake for 5 minutes. Remove from the oven, garnish with chopped parsley and serve immediately. ♜

Shallow individual porcelain gratin dishes make this recipe easy to prepare and serve. For the most attractive and traditional presentation, however, look for large natural scallop shells from the sea in specialty-cookware shops or high-quality fishmongers. Each shell is just the right size for one serving.

POTAGE BONNE FEMME

SERVES 4

I find it interesting that as our knowledge of French cooking grew more sophisticated, we began to appreciate French provincial favorites, such as this "good woman's" version of leek-and-potato soup. If you purée and chill the soup, then enrich it with a little more cream and adjust the seasonings to taste, you will end up with the elegant cold soup known as vichyssoise, which is largely unknown in France and was actually invented in New York in 1910 by French chef Louis Diat.

1 bunch leeks (3 or 4 medium)
2 tablespoons unsalted butter
3 small carrots, peeled and diced
1 lb baking potatoes, peeled and diced
5 cups water
pinch of sugar
salt and freshly ground pepper
⅓ cup (3 fl oz) heavy cream
chopped fresh parsley

TRIM THE LEEKS, leaving about 1 inch of the tender green tops intact. Remove and discard any old leaves. Make a lengthwise slit along each leek to within about 2 inches of the root end. Hold each leek under cold running water and separate the leaves slightly to rinse away any dirt lodged between the layers. Slice the leeks thinly.

IN A SAUCEPAN over medium heat, melt the butter. When hot, add the leeks and carrots and sauté until softened, about 3 minutes. Add the potatoes, water, sugar and salt and pepper to taste. Bring to a boil, reduce the heat to medium-low, cover partially and cook until the vegetables are tender, about 30 minutes.

REMOVE FROM THE HEAT and pass the mixture through the fine disk of a food mill into a clean saucepan (or use a fine-mesh sieve). Reheat gently over low heat. Add the cream and taste and adjust the seasonings. Ladle into warmed bowls and sprinkle with parsley. Serve immediately. ⚜

Basic Vegetable Soup

It seems to me that one of the first things people learn when they are determined to become good cooks is how easy it is to make good soup from scratch. Here's a very basic recipe.

Peel and finely dice onions, leeks, potatoes, carrots and celery in quantities and combinations defined by the number of people you are feeding and the vegetables you have on hand. Sauté the onions and leeks in unsalted butter until golden—this is important, the secret of Good Soup—in a deep pot. Add the rest of the diced vegetables with enough water or chicken stock to cover, and throw in some salt. Bring to the boil and then simmer for about 25 minutes, or until the vegetables are tender. Reduce the vegetables to a purée in a food mill, blender or food processor fitted with the metal blade. Return to the pot, heat through and adjust seasonings. Stir in a little cream and chopped parsley. This should be a fairly thick soup. Accompany with crusty French bread.

"Simple is the password in cooking today: If food is not simple, it is not good. But, unless the supremely social acts of eating and drinking, of human communion at table, of analyzing and sharing voluptuous experience evolved and refined within the nonetheless flexible boundaries of tradition, find their place as primordial and essential threads in the larger fabric of simplicity, Simple Food as a concept can have no meaning beyond that of elementary nourishment for the anti-sensualist or ease of preparation for the lazy cook."

—Richard Olney,
Simple French Food (1974)

SOLE BONNE FEMME

SERVES 4

Although it is baked in the oven, this very simple French country dish is actually poached, a cooking method that started growing in use in the late 1960s. The thin sole fillets simmer and steam in the little bit of white wine you pour over them in their baking dish, as well as in the liquid that exudes from their bed of mushrooms and shallots. That cooking liquid is then reduced to an essence that flavors the hollandaise sauce used for glazing the fish.

2 shallots, finely chopped
4 fresh mushrooms, wiped clean and thinly sliced
1 tablespoon chopped fresh parsley
4 sole fillets, 6–8 oz each
¼ cup (2 fl oz) dry white wine
salt and freshly ground pepper

FOR THE HOLLANDAISE SAUCE:
2 egg yolks
1 tablespoon water
½ cup (4 oz) unsalted butter, at room temperature,
  cut into small cubes
salt and white pepper
fresh lemon juice

PREHEAT AN OVEN to 375°F. Generously butter a flameproof baking dish just large enough to hold the fillets in a single layer.

SPRINKLE THE SHALLOTS, mushrooms and half of the parsley evenly over the bottom of the prepared dish. Lay the sole fillets over the vegetables, tucking the thin ends under to ensure even cooking, then pour the white wine over the fish. Season to taste with salt and pepper and cover with a piece of buttered brown paper (not from a recycled paper bag), parchment paper or aluminum foil.

BAKE UNTIL THE FISH IS OPAQUE THROUGHOUT, 10–15 minutes; do not overcook.

REMOVE FROM THE OVEN. Holding the fish in place with a slotted spoon, drain off the liquid into a small saucepan. Keep the fish warm. Place the saucepan over high heat and boil until reduced by about three-fourths; you should have 3–4 tablespoons. Set aside.

TO MAKE THE HOLLANDAISE, place the egg yolks and water in a heatproof bowl or in the top pan of a double boiler over (but not touching) simmering water in a saucepan or the bottom pan of the double boiler. Whisk together the egg yolks and water until warm and just beginning to thicken, about 1 minute. While continuing to whisk, add the butter a little at a time until all of it is incorporated and the sauce has thickened, 2–3 minutes. (Do not cook the mixture too long or the eggs will curdle.) Remove the bowl or pan from over the water to stop the cooking, and season the sauce to taste with salt and pepper and a few drops of lemon juice.

PREHEAT A BROILER. Add the reserved reduced liquid to the hollandaise sauce and stir to mix well. Pour evenly over the fish in the baking dish. Place under the broiler about 3 inches from the heat and broil until lightly glazed, just a minute or so. Do not allow to boil, or the sauce will separate.

GARNISH WITH THE REMAINING PARSLEY and serve immediately, directly from the baking dish. ✿

> ## Elizabeth David's Garlic Sauce
>
> *In a mortar, pound a clove or two of garlic; add a handful of bread crumbs, enough olive oil to make a thick sauce and a little vinegar. Serve with any coarse white fish that is fried, baked or poached.*

"Rules vary depending on the lawmakers; some claim that only fresh-water fish should be treated in court bouillon, salt-water fish being poached in salt water; furthermore, different court bouillons are often recommended for different fish. As far as I'm concerned, fresh fish of any sort is good poached in salt water; it is better if a bay leaf and a branch of thyme are added; and it is best if treated in a wine court bouillon, the specific proportions of the ingredients not being important."

—Richard Olney, *Simple French Food* (1977)

POACHED SALMON

SERVES 4–6

A whole fish makes a spectacular hot or cold main course for a dinner party or buffet. This particular recipe, however, makes use of a 2-pound piece, which fits in a good-sized saucepan. You could triple the recipe and pull out your fish poacher (see opposite) if you want to serve a whole fish, as shown. When cooking a smaller portion, I like the tail section, which I feel has a better flavor and texture. If you like, offer a hollandaise sauce (recipe on page 72) with the salmon, or a green mayonnaise flavored with finely chopped fresh parsley or tarragon.

1 cup (8 fl oz) dry white wine
5 cups water
1 large yellow onion, sliced
1 large carrot, peeled and sliced
2 fresh thyme sprigs
1 celery stalk, sliced
6–8 fresh parsley sprigs
2 tablespoons sea salt
6–8 peppercorns
1 bay leaf
1 piece salmon tail end with skin and bone intact, 2 lb
1 lemon, cut into wedges

SELECT A SAUCEPAN or deep sauté pan in which the salmon will fit comfortably. Add the wine, water, onion, carrot, thyme, celery, half of the parsley sprigs, the sea salt, peppercorns and bay leaf and place over medium-high heat. Bring just to a boil, reduce the heat to medium and simmer, uncovered, for 20–30 minutes to make a full-flavored bouillon.

PLACE THE FISH on its side on a flat work surface and measure the fish at its thickest point. Determine the poaching time by allowing 10 minutes for each 1 inch of thickness.

CUT A PIECE OF CHEESECLOTH about 20 inches long. Lay the fish across the middle of the cheesecloth. Have the bouillon barely at a simmer. Holding the two ends of the cheesecloth, carefully lower the salmon into the bouillon; lay the ends of the cheesecloth on top so that they remain accessible. The bouillon should just cover the fish; if it does not, add hot water as needed.

COVER AND BARELY SIMMER, with only a few bubbles rising in the water, for the determined time. To test for doneness, stick the tip of a knife into the thickest part of the fish; the flesh at the center should be opaque.

TURN OFF THE HEAT and let the fish rest in the bouillon for about 5 minutes. With the aid of the cheesecloth, carefully lift out the fish and place on a warmed platter, slipping the cheesecloth free. Carefully peel off the skin from the top side of the salmon and discard. Gently turn the salmon over and peel off the skin from the opposite side. Using a thin knife, loosen the flesh from the bone to make it easier to serve. Garnish with the lemon wedges and remaining parsley sprigs. 🐚

FISH POACHERS

By the early 1970s, if you were at all serious about cooking, you had to have a fish poacher. These long, narrow metal pans contain perforated metal racks that make it easy to lift out a whole poached fish in one piece. The poachers come in two or three sizes, some large enough to cover two burners on your stove, and are made of copper, stainless steel or aluminum.

MEAT LOAF

SERVES 6–8

1 tablespoon unsalted butter
1 yellow onion, finely chopped
1 celery stalk, finely chopped
¼–⅓ cup (2–3 fl oz) milk, or as needed
1½ cups (6 oz) medium-fine bread crumbs,
  preferably made from day-old French bread
1½ lb ground lean beef (chuck or round)
½ lb ground veal
½ lb ground pork
2 eggs
2 tablespoons chopped fresh parsley
1 teaspoon chopped fresh thyme or ½ teaspoon dried thyme
1½ teaspoons salt
freshly ground pepper

PREHEAT AN OVEN to 350°F. Butter a 9-by-5-inch loaf pan.

IN A FRYING PAN over medium heat, melt the butter. Add the onion and celery and sauté until the onion is translucent, 3–5 minutes; do not allow to brown. Remove from the heat and set aside.

IN A BOWL, dribble the milk a little at a time over the bread crumbs, stirring with a fork just until lightly and evenly moistened. Let stand until the crumbs have absorbed the liquid, about 5 minutes. Add the sautéed onion and celery, beef, veal, pork, eggs, parsley, thyme, salt and pepper to taste. Using your hands or a fork, mix until well blended and the meat is evenly distributed.

SPOON THE MEAT MIXTURE loosely into the prepared loaf pan. Do not pack it down. Smooth and round off the top.

BAKE UNTIL COOKED THROUGH to the center and the juices run clear when pierced with a knife, or until an instant-read thermom-eter inserted into the center registers 160°F, 1–1½ hours. Remove from the oven and let rest for 5 minutes. Pour off any juices into a bowl. Spoon the fat off the juices, then strain the juices and reserve. Turn out the meat loaf, right side up, onto a platter. Slice to serve, then use the juices to moisten the meat loaf. 🦪

STEAK AU POIVRE WITH BEARNAISE SAUCE

SERVES 4

4 slices lean bacon
4 slices beef fillet, each about 5–6 oz, 3 inches wide and
  1–1½ inches thick
2–3 tablespoons coarsely cracked peppercorns (see right)
¼ cup (2 fl oz) tarragon vinegar
2 shallots, finely chopped
2 egg yolks
1 tablespoon heavy cream
2 teaspoons chopped fresh tarragon
½ cup (4 oz) unsalted butter, cut into small cubes, plus
  2 tablespoons unsalted butter
salt
1 tablespoon vegetable oil

WRAP A SLICE OF BACON around the circumference of each fillet and secure in place with kitchen string. Sprinkle both sides of each fillet with the peppercorns and pat firmly into the meat. Set aside.

IN A SMALL SAUCEPAN over medium-high heat, combine the vinegar and shallots. Bring to a boil and cook until only about 1 teaspoon liquid remains; do not allow to burn. Let cool slightly.

IN A BOWL, whisk together the egg yolks, cream and half of the tarragon. Add to the saucepan holding the reduced liquid. Place or hold over (but not touching) simmering water in another saucepan. Whisk until beginning to thicken. Add the ½ cup butter, cube by cube, whisking after each addition until completely incorporated, then continue whisking until thick. Season to taste with salt. Cover and place over the hot water off the heat to keep warm until needed.

IN A HEAVY FRYING PAN over medium-high heat, melt the 2 tablespoons butter with the vegetable oil. When hot, season the fillets with salt and add to the pan. Fry, turning once, until browned on both sides, 4–5 minutes on each side for medium-rare. Then turn the fillets on their sides and lightly brown the bacon while turning, 1–2 minutes. Transfer to warmed individual plates and snip and remove the strings. Spoon the warm sauce over the fillets and sprinkle the remaining tarragon evenly over the tops. Serve at once. ☙

CRACKING PEPPERCORNS

Of course, you can easily crack whole peppercorns yourself. Put them in a plastic bag on the kitchen counter and hit them gently with something heavy; I used a milk bottle back before cardboard cartons were common, but the bottom of a heavy pan will do. Keep an eye on the peppercorns, hitting a few at a time until you get the right force. You want each one broken into four or five pieces.

PORC A L'ORANGE

SERVES 4–6

In the late 1960s, nearly everyone came to know the French dish canard
à l'orange, *"duck with orange sauce," but duck was and still is an expensive, special-occasion ingredient. I found the original version of this recipe
in* Les recettes de Mapie, *a collection of recipes published in 1956 by
the Comtesse Guy de Toulouse-Lautrec. Not long after I feebly translated
and adapted the recipe and tried it on some friends, it spread around the
dinner-party circuit in the Bay Area. Because it is naturally sweet and
rich, pork works very well with the orange sauce. Although the recipe calls
for a whole stick of butter, you'll notice that most of the fat is skimmed
away when finishing the sauce.*

½ cup (4 oz) unsalted butter, cut into small cubes
1 pork loin, bones removed and trimmed of fat, 2½–3 lb
4 carrots, peeled and thinly sliced
1 teaspoon chopped fresh thyme or ½ teaspoon dried thyme
1 bay leaf
¼ cup (2 fl oz) Cognac or other high-quality brandy
1 cup (8 fl oz) dry white wine, warmed slightly
salt and freshly ground pepper
3 oranges

IN A SMALL SAUCEPAN over very low heat, melt the butter, watching carefully so it does not burn. Remove from the heat and let stand for a minute to settle, then carefully skim off the foam from the top and discard. Pour the remaining yellow liquid into a cup, leaving the milky solids behind in the pan. The clear yellow liquid is clarified butter. Discard the milky solids.

TRANSFER THE CLARIFIED BUTTER to a heavy 4-quart saucepan or sauté pan just large enough to hold the meat easily. Place over medium heat and, when hot, add the pork and brown well on all sides, 8–10 minutes total. Transfer to a plate.

ADD THE CARROTS to the saucepan over medium heat and toss until lightly browned, 2–3 minutes. Add the thyme and bay leaf and return the meat to the saucepan. Pour the brandy into a ladle, heat over a burner on the stove and ignite carefully with a match away from the burner. Pour over the meat. When the flames die down, pour the wine over the meat as well and add salt and pepper to taste. Reduce the heat to medium-low, cover and simmer until the meat is very tender, about 2 hours. Remove the pork from the pan and set aside on a plate. Keep warm. Discard the bay leaf.

USING A LARGE SPOON, skim the fat from the meat juices and discard. Bring the juices to a boil over high heat and boil until reduced to about 1 cup. Meanwhile, using a zester, remove the zest from 1 orange in fine shreds. Alternatively, using a small, sharp knife, remove the orange zest in wide strips and cut into tiny strips. Bring a small saucepan three-fourths full of water to a boil, add the zest strips and boil for 2 minutes. Drain well. Squeeze the juice from the orange and add to the reduced juices along with the drained zest. Simmer, uncovered, over medium low heat for 3–4 minutes to blend the flavors.

CUT THE REMAINING 2 ORANGES into slices ¼ inch thick. Arrange around the rim of a warmed serving platter. Place the pork in the center and pour the sauce over it. Carve and serve. ♛

> "Entertaining, and entertaining well, is possible for everyone, because it is not the money spent that assures success of a party—lunch, dinner or cocktail—but the effort, the originality, the taste with which it has been prepared."
>
> —Mapie, Comtesse Guy de Toulouse-Lautrec, *Les recettes de Mapie* (1956)

LAMB AND ZUCCHINI MOUSSAKA

SERVES 4

4 or 5 zucchini
salt
3–4 tablespoons olive oil
1 yellow onion, chopped
1 clove garlic, chopped
1 lb ground lamb
1 teaspoon chopped fresh oregano or ½ teaspoon dried oregano
2 eggs, lightly beaten
3 tomatoes, peeled, seeded (see page 70) and finely chopped
¼ cup (1 oz) freshly grated Parmesan or Romano cheese
1 cup (2 oz) fresh bread crumbs
¼ cup (2 fl oz) chicken stock or tomato juice

CUT THE ZUCCHINI lengthwise into slices ¼ inch thick. Arrange the slices in a colander placed in a sink or over a bowl, overlapping them as little as possible. Sprinkle with salt and let the bitter juices drain off for 1 hour. Rinse and pat dry with paper towels.

PREHEAT AN OVEN to 375°F. Butter a 10-by-8½-by-2½-inch baking dish.

IN A SAUTÉ PAN or frying pan over medium heat, warm 3 tablespoons olive oil. When hot, add the zucchini and sauté, turning as needed, until lightly browned on both sides, about 5 minutes total. Do this in two batches if necessary to avoid crowding the pan, adding more oil if needed. Using a slotted spoon or spatula, transfer to a plate and set aside.

ADD THE ONION and garlic to the same pan and sauté over medium heat until translucent, 5–7 minutes. Add the lamb, breaking it up with a fork, and brown lightly, 3–4 minutes.

POUR OFF any accumulated fat. Season to taste with salt and the oregano. Remove from the heat and let cool a little. Stir the eggs into the meat mixture. Set aside.

ARRANGE HALF OF THE SAUTÉED ZUCCHINI in a single layer in the prepared baking dish, overlapping the slices if necessary. Cover evenly with the meat mixture, and then the tomatoes. Arrange the remaining zucchini slices in a single layer on top, again overlapping if necessary. In a small bowl, stir together the cheese and bread crumbs and sprinkle evenly over the zucchini. Drizzle the stock or tomato juice over the crumbs to moisten.

BAKE UNTIL THE MIXTURE is cooked through and the top is browned, about 35 minutes. Remove from the oven and let stand for a few minutes, then serve directly from the dish. ✿

CHICKEN IN A CLAY POT

SERVES 4

In the late 1960s, Williams-Sonoma began to import unglazed terra-cotta baking pots from Italy and England, reviving a centuries-old Etruscan cooking method that works well for chicken, veal, pork or ham.

1 chicken, about 3 lb
sea salt and freshly ground pepper
½ lemon
1 or 2 cloves garlic
2 or 3 fresh sage leaves
1 fresh rosemary sprig
1 small carrot
2 small celery stalks
¼ cup (2 fl oz) dry white wine
1 yellow onion, thinly sliced

PREHEAT AN OVEN to 375°F.

RINSE THE CHICKEN inside and out and pat dry with paper towels. Sprinkle the cavity with sea salt and pepper to taste. Squeeze a little of the juice from the lemon half into the cavity and then leave the lemon half in the cavity. Tuck the garlic, sage, rosemary, carrot and celery into the cavity and pour in the wine. Arrange the onion slices on the bottom of an unglazed terra-cotta chicken pot, covering completely. Place the chicken on top, breast side up, and cover with the pot lid.

BAKE UNTIL THE CHICKEN is tender and the juices run clear, or until an instant-read thermometer inserted into the thickest part of the thigh away from the bone registers 180°F, about 1½ hours.

TRANSFER TO A WARMED PLATTER and let stand for a few minutes, then carve and serve. ✿

VEAL PAPRIKA WITH SPATZLE

SERVES 6

French and Italian dishes weren't the only foreign foods American home cooks were discovering in the late 1960s and early 1970s. Eastern Europe was opening up to visitors, and its cuisines were also making an impression, reinforced by the cooking of Eastern European immigrants and their descendants. At Williams-Sonoma, we started to carry good Hungarian paprika, which is much more flavorful than what is found in the small tins available in most supermarkets. And we imported a spätzle sieve (see opposite) for making the tiny dumplings that go so well with veal paprika.

FOR THE VEAL PAPRIKA:
2 tablespoons unsalted butter
2 tablespoons vegetable oil
1 yellow onion, minced
1 clove garlic, chopped
2 teaspoons sweet or hot paprika
2½ lb veal shoulder, trimmed of fat and cut into 1-inch cubes
2 tomatoes, peeled, seeded and chopped (see left)
2 fresh Anaheim chili peppers, seeded and sliced
3 tablespoons water

Peeling and Seeding Tomatoes

Bring a saucepan three-fourths full of water to a boil. Meanwhile, using a small, sharp knife, cut out the core from the stem end of each tomato, then cut a shallow X in the blossom end. Slip the tomatoes into the boiling water for 20 seconds, then transfer to a bowl of cold water. When cool, starting at the X, slip off the skins. Cut each tomato in half crosswise and squeeze out the seeds. Cut as directed in individual recipes.

70

salt and freshly ground pepper
1½ cups (12 fl oz) sour cream
1 cup (8 fl oz) heavy cream
2 tablespoons all-purpose flour

FOR THE SPATZLE:
1½ teaspoons salt
3 eggs
¾ cup (6 fl oz) water
2¼ cups (11½ oz) all-purpose flour
pinch of freshly grated nutmeg
½ teaspoon baking powder
⅓ cup (1½ oz) freshly grated Parmesan cheese
¼ cup (2 oz) unsalted butter, melted

TO MAKE THE VEAL PAPRIKA, in a large frying pan over medium-low heat, melt the butter with the vegetable oil. When hot, add the onion and garlic and sauté until translucent, 7–10 minutes. Stir in the paprika and cook, stirring, for another 30 seconds. Add the veal cubes to the pan, raise the heat to medium-high and sauté until lightly browned, about 15 minutes. Add the tomatoes, chili peppers, water and salt and pepper to taste. Mix well, reduce the heat to medium and cook, stirring occasionally, until the veal is tender, 20–25 minutes. In a bowl, stir together the sour cream, heavy cream and flour. Set aside.

WHILE THE VEAL IS COOKING, make the spätzle: Bring a large pot two-thirds full of water to a boil and add 1 teaspoon of the salt. In a large bowl, beat the eggs until well blended. Add the water, flour, nutmeg, baking powder and the remaining ½ teaspoon salt, beating until well mixed. Using a spätzle maker, a colander with large holes (about ¼ inch) or a handheld shredder with large holes, force the batter through the holes into the boiling water. (If using a colander or shredder, push the batter through the holes with a rubber spatula.) Stir the spätzle to prevent them from sticking together and boil until tender, about 3 minutes. The spätzle will swell and rise to the surface. Drain thoroughly and place in a warmed bowl. Add the cheese and melted butter and toss well. Keep warm.

STIR THE SOUR CREAM MIXTURE into the veal and cook over medium heat for a few minutes until thickened. Taste and adjust the seasonings. Serve with the spätzle. ♛

THE SPATZLE MAKER

The perforated rectangular metal plate of a spätzle maker resembles a shredder with holes that are the perfect size for shaping the tiny dumplings. You rest the device on top of a pot of boiling water and put the spätzle batter into its sliding box. Pushing the box back and forth forces the batter through the holes into the water, forming teardrop-shaped dumplings. In the absense of a spätzle maker, use a rubber spatula to push the batter through the holes of a colander or handheld shredder.

DOUBLE BOILERS

The hollandaise sauce in this recipe, as well as chocolate or custard sauces or other preparations or foods that might suffer from too much direct heat, benefits from being cooked in a double boiler, a pair of stacked saucepans that includes a lid that fits either pan. Water simmered in the lower pan provides gentle heat to cook the contents of the upper pan. The water, however, must never be so deep as to touch the bottom of the upper pan. Double boilers come in many shapes, sizes and materials—aluminum, copper, enameled steel, stainless steel and heatproof glass— and most are designed so that each section can also be used separately as a saucepan. Copper double boilers generally have ceramic upper inserts with brass collars and handles; although less versatile, they are attractive. You can also find double-boiler inserts that fit over pots you may already own, or you can improvise a double boiler by resting a slightly larger pan with rounded sides, or a heatproof bowl, over a smaller pan of simmering water.

EGGS BENEDICT

SERVES 6

Ever since the 1920s, when it was reputedly developed by the chef at Delmonico's Restaurant in New York, this brunch dish of English muffins topped with Canadian bacon, poached eggs and hollandaise sauce has been enjoyed by Americans. When hollandaise sauce became popular again in this country during the late 1960s, it was only natural that eggs benedict experienced a new vogue as well.

FOR THE HOLLANDAISE SAUCE:
3 egg yolks
½ teaspoon salt
1 tablespoon fresh lemon juice
½ cup (4 oz) unsalted butter, at room temperature, cut into
  small cubes

1 tablespoon vinegar
1 teaspoon salt
6 eggs
6 slices Canadian bacon
1 tablespoon unsalted butter
3 English muffins, split, toasted and buttered
chopped fresh parsley
drained capers

TO MAKE THE HOLLANDAISE, put the egg yolks, salt and lemon juice in a heatproof bowl or in the top of a double boiler over (but not touching) simmering water in a saucepan or the bottom pan of the double boiler. Whisk them together until warm and just beginning to thicken, about 1 minute. While continuing to whisk, add the butter a little at a time until all of it is incorporated and the sauce has thickened, 2–3 minutes. (Do not cook the mixture too long or the eggs will curdle.) It should have the consistency of heavy cream. To keep the sauce warm until the rest of the ingredients are ready, place the bowl or pan, covered, over warm water off the heat.

IN A LARGE FRYING PAN or sauté pan, pour in water to a depth of 1½ inches. Add the vinegar and salt and bring to a boil. Reduce the heat so that the liquid is barely simmering, with just a few bubbles rising to the surface. Break an egg into a saucer and gently slip the egg into the water. Repeat with the remaining eggs, spacing well apart. Cook the eggs, spooning a little of the hot water over the yolks, until the whites are firm and the yolks are glazed but still liquid, 3–5 minutes.

CAREFULLY REMOVE THE EGGS with a skimmer, a large slotted spoon or a slotted spatula and place on a paper towel–lined flat plate to drain. Trim the edges of the egg whites if they are ragged.

WHILE THE EGGS ARE COOKING, trim the Canadian bacon slices to fit the English muffins. In a large frying pan or sauté pan over medium heat, melt the butter. Add the bacon slices and sauté, turning once, to heat through, 2–3 minutes total. Remove from the heat.

PLACE 1 MUFFIN HALF, buttered side up, on each individual plate and top each with a slice of the bacon and then with an egg. Spoon the hollandaise sauce over the eggs, dividing it evenly. Sprinkle with parsley and garnish with a few capers. Serve at once. ҉

Spinach Frittata

Having mastered the omelet in our early explorations of French cooking, we soon discovered how good the rustic flat omelets of France and Italy could be. Here's one created for our catalog:

Using a large sauté pan, brown ¼ lb ground beef in 1 tablespoon olive oil, crumbling the meat with a fork. Stir in 2 cups (4 oz) rinsed, dried and finely chopped spinach and steam, covered, for a minute or two; let cool for 5 minutes. (Or substitute one package (10-oz) frozen spinach, thawed, which will not require steaming.) Stir in 4 eggs, lightly beaten; 1 cup (4 oz) shredded sharp Cheddar cheese; ¼ cup (2 fl oz) dry red wine; 2 tablespoons fine dried bread crumbs and ½ teaspoon salt. Turn into a buttered 9-by-6-inch baking dish and top with a dusting of grated Parmesan cheese. Bake at 375°F until golden brown, about 45 minutes. Cut into squares and serve hot or cold for lunch or as an hors d'oeuvre. Serves 2.

ONE TRICK I LEARNED

ONE TRICK I LEARNED for getting a higher rise to a soufflé, beyond that of using a copper bowl to help beat more air into the whites (see page 44), is adding a little liquor. (Here, I use Madeira, which complements the flavor of the shrimp.) Because the alcohol evaporates at a lower temperature than water, it produces vapors that give the eggs an extra lift.

SHRIMP SOUFFLE

SERVES 4

The soufflé craze just kept growing stronger into the 1970s, with new recipes appearing every month. This recipe is a good example of how cooks progressed beyond the basic cheese soufflé (page 44). Crab meat or chopped cooked chicken may be substituted for the shrimp.

10 oz shrimp, peeled and deveined
½ cup (4 fl oz) heavy cream
½ cup (4 fl oz) milk
2 tablespoons unsalted butter
2 tablespoons all-purpose flour
4 egg yolks
½ teaspoon salt
pinch of cayenne pepper
freshly ground black pepper
1 tablespoon Madeira wine
1 tablespoon fresh lemon juice
5 egg whites

PREHEAT AN OVEN to 350°F. Select a 1½-quart soufflé dish. Using parchment paper or aluminum foil, make a collar for the dish (see page 44). Do not grease the collar or the dish.

BRING A SAUCEPAN three-fourths full of water to a boil. Add the shrimp and cook until they turn pink and curl, 3–4 minutes. Drain and, when cool enough to handle, chop finely. You should have about 1 cup. Set aside.

IN ANOTHER SAUCEPAN over medium-low heat, combine the cream and milk and heat just until bubbles appear around the edges of the pan. Remove from the heat and set aside. In a separate saucepan over medium-low heat, melt the butter. When hot, add the flour and, using a whisk, stir until blended, then cook, stirring vigorously for 2 minutes; do not allow to brown. Gradually pour the cream-and-milk mixture into the flour mixture, whisking constantly. Raise the heat to medium and continue to cook, stirring constantly, until the sauce is smooth, thick and comes to a boil, 2–3 minutes. Cook for a few seconds longer until fully thickened, then remove from the heat and let cool for 5 minutes.

IN A BOWL, whisk the egg yolks until pale yellow, 1–2 minutes. Add a little of the hot sauce to the yolks and beat until blended, then gradually stir the yolks into the sauce. Add the shrimp and season with the salt, cayenne pepper, black pepper to taste, Madeira and lemon juice. Stir to mix well.

IN A CLEAN, DRY BOWL, and using a clean whisk or an electric mixer, beat the egg whites until soft peaks form. Spoon about one-fourth of the egg whites into the sauce and, using a rubber spatula, stir gently to blend and lighten the mixture. Scoop the remaining egg whites on top of the sauce and fold them in gently just until no white streaks remain. Spoon the mixture into the prepared soufflé dish.

BAKE UNTIL PUFFED and lightly browned, about 35 minutes. Remove from the oven and carefully remove the collar. Serve at once. ※

COLCANNON

SERVES 4

1½ lb baking potatoes, peeled and quartered
salt
3–4 cups (9–12 oz) coarsely chopped green cabbage
½–⅔ cup (4–5 fl oz) milk, heated
2 green onions, including tender green tops, sliced lengthwise and
  then cut crosswise into 1-inch shreds
freshly ground pepper

PLACE THE POTATOES in a saucepan with water to cover generously and salt to taste. Place over medium-high heat, bring to a boil and cook until just tender, 15–20 minutes.

MEANWHILE, bring a saucepan three-fourths full of water to a boil. Add the cabbage and boil for 2–3 minutes. Drain well.

WHEN THE POTATOES ARE READY, drain and return to the saucepan. Using a potato masher, mash until fluffy. Gradually beat in enough milk to make them smooth. Place the pan over low heat and add the cabbage, onions and salt and pepper to taste. Mix well and heat through. Transfer to a warmed serving dish and serve at once. ※

GIVE CREDIT for this peasant dish to the Irish, who showed Americans that another good way to make mashed potatoes was to mix them with other vegetables. It would be just as good an accompaniment to steak au poivre (recipe page 65) or chicken in a clay pot (recipe page 69) as it would to a humble meat loaf (recipe page 64).

CHUCK'S ZUCCHINI

SERVES 6

15–20 very small zucchini
salt
½ lemon

TRIM THE UNPEELED ZUCCHINI and shred on the small or me-dium holes of a handheld shredder, a crank-type European shredder (see left) or the medium- or fine-holed disk of a food processor.

PUT THE ZUCCHINI into a large sauté pan, cover and place over high heat for 20–30 seconds. Uncover and stir, adjusting the heat as needed so the zucchini does not burn. Re-cover, let steam again for 10–20 seconds, then uncover and stir. Repeat until the zucchini is just heated through; it should remain crisp and green. If too much juice appears, leave off the cover to reduce the liquid. The whole process should only take a few minutes.

JUST BEFORE SERVING, add salt to taste and a squeeze of lemon juice. Transfer to a warmed serving dish and serve immediately. ☙

IT WAS OFTEN JOKED that I had come up with over a hundred different ways to cook zucchini, so wide-spread did they become and so quickly did they overrun people's gardens. This is one of the easiest. It originally called for a Mouli Julienne, a hand-cranked shredder that was a popular import from France.

Of course, since the time I wrote this recipe, the food processor has superseded the hand-powered tool in the speed with which it can shred great quantities of vegetables.

76

BRUSSELS SPROUTS WITH MUSTARD

SERVES 4

True Dijon mustard is made in Dijon, France, from dark brown mustard seeds (unless otherwise marked blanc) *blended with white wine or wine vinegar. It is pale yellow and has a fairly hot and sharp flavor. Its use here, blended with sour cream to make a sauce for Brussels sprouts, shows off the mustard's versatility.*

1 lb small Brussels sprouts
1 tablespoon salt
2 tablespoons Dijon mustard
2 tablespoons sour cream

TRIM THE STEMS and remove any wilted or yellowed leaves from the Brussels sprouts. Cut a cross in the stem end of each sprout and place in a bowl with water to cover generously. Let stand for 15 minutes.

BRING A SAUCEPAN three-fourths full of water to a boil over high heat and add the salt. Drain the sprouts and add to the boiling water. Cover partially and cook until just tender, about 10 minutes.

DRAIN WELL and return to the saucepan. In a small bowl or cup, stir together the mustard and sour cream. Add to the sprouts and toss until well coated. Transfer to a warmed serving dish and serve immediately. ♛

DIJON MUSTARD

Sometime in the late 1960s, large, beautifully labeled stoneware crocks of mustard suddenly appeared in French food stores in the United States. The lovely wine-, vinegar- and spice-infused Dijon mustard, a favorite of connoisseurs and long a standard condiment on royal tables, had been made by Pommery since 1632. In short supply on its emergence after World War II, Elizabeth David told me, "If you see a jar of it, grab it." I did, and we had a wonderful mustard Christmas that year selling hundreds of jars in the Williams-Sonoma shop. Although Pommery is still not easy to find, I believe it played an important role in the Dijon-mustard invasion of America.

"Spoon bread, accord-
ing to legend, was
created when a mix-
ture used to make
corn bread enriched
by milk and eggs was
left forgotten in a hot
oven. Virginians claim
this happened in one
of *their* kitchens, and
as a consequence
spoon bread has been
one of their favored
foods ever since."

—Bernard Clayton Jr., *The
Complete Book of Breads* (1973)

SPOON BREAD

SERVES 4

*I'm sure the interest in soufflés is what led Americans to rediscover this
traditional recipe from the American South. Serve as an accompaniment
to any dish that has a lot of good gravy.*

1½ cups (12 fl oz) milk
freshly grated nutmeg
1 teaspoon salt
¾ cup (4 oz) yellow cornmeal
2 tablespoons unsalted butter, melted
3 egg yolks, lightly beaten
1 teaspoon baking powder
2 tablespoons freshly grated Parmesan cheese
4 egg whites

PREHEAT AN OVEN to 425°F. Butter a 1½-quart soufflé dish or
other deep baking dish.

POUR THE MILK into a saucepan and add a little nutmeg and the
salt. Place over medium heat and heat until small bubbles appear
around the edges of the pan; do not allow to boil. Remove from the
heat. Then, while stirring vigorously, slowly add the cornmeal to the
milk. Continue to beat until smooth. Stir in the melted butter, egg
yolks, baking powder and grated cheese, mixing well.

IN A BOWL, using a whisk or electric mixer, beat the egg whites
until soft peaks form. Using a rubber spatula, gently fold the egg
whites into the cornmeal mixture. Pour into the prepared dish.

BAKE FOR 10 MINUTES. Reduce the heat to 375°F and bake until
the top is puffed, set and golden, about 20 minutes longer. Serve
at once.

BUTTERMILK POPOVERS

MAKES 6–9 POPOVERS, DEPENDING UPON SIZE OF CUPS

These homey, light-as-air little American breads, an old-fashioned specialty of the Deep South, were being rediscovered by cooks in the early 1970s. They're great for brunch, or as a side dish with a dinner roast, served just as you would England's Yorkshire pudding. To encourage them to rise fully, use a pan with deep cups and heat it up in the preheated oven before you add the batter.

1 cup (5 oz) all-purpose flour
¼ teaspoon salt
3 eggs
1 cup (8 fl oz) buttermilk
1 tablespoon unsalted butter, melted,
  plus 6–9 teaspoons unsalted butter

PREHEAT AN OVEN to 425°F.

IN A BOWL, sift together the flour and salt. Add the eggs, buttermilk and the 1 tablespoon melted butter and, using a whisk or wooden spoon, beat vigorously until mixture is the consistency of heavy cream, about 2 minutes.

PUT ABOUT 1 TEASPOON BUTTER into each popover cup and place in the oven for a few seconds until the butter is bubbling. Remove from the oven and fill each cup half full of batter. Return to the oven and bake for 20 minutes. Reduce the heat to 325°F and bake until the popovers are nicely browned and well risen above the rims of the cups, 15–20 minutes longer. To keep the popovers from deflating, remove from the oven and quickly pierce each one with a thin skewer to let the air escape, then return them to the oven for a few seconds. Serve immediately. ♔

Although you could make popovers in a muffin tin, true popover pans have extra-deep cups that let the popovers rise higher. Traditional versions were made of cast iron and had 11 cups. Newer popover pans have tinned or black steel cups supported on a wire frame that allows the oven's heat to circulate around each popover for even airier results.

Other Uses for Kugelhopf

Slices of freshly baked kugelhopf are wonderful with a cup of tea or coffee. The loaf will keep well for several days if stored at cool room temperature, sealed in an airtight container or plastic bag. To freshen the flavor, try toasting the slices lightly under the broiler, keeping them 8–10 inches from the heat so they won't burn. Slices of leftover kugelhopf may also be dipped in beaten egg and fried in butter to make French toast. Or they can be transformed into an elegant dessert: First, simmer a mixture of 1 cup water and ¹/₂ cup (4 oz) sugar for 10 minutes, then let cool slightly and stir in ¹/₂ cup (4 fl oz) dark rum. Place slices of the kugelhopf on individual serving plates and soak them liberally with the warm syrup, then top with whipped cream.

ORANGE KUGELHOPF

MAKES 1 COFFEE CAKE; SERVES 8

Over the years, Williams-Sonoma has sold six or seven different versions of the fluted pan used for baking this traditional Alsatian yeast-leavened tea bread. I think the pan's popularity demonstrates how people who love to bake are attracted to new shapes in baking pans. For an added touch, dust with confectioners' sugar before serving.

½ cup (3 oz) golden raisins
1 tablespoon dry sherry
3 cups (15 oz) all-purpose flour
¼ teaspoon salt
½ cup (4 oz) sugar
1 package (2½ teaspoons) active dry yeast
3 eggs
¾ cup (6 fl oz) milk, warmed (110°F)
finely grated zest of 1 orange
1 teaspoon vanilla extract
¾ cup (6 oz) unsalted butter, at room temperature, cut into small pieces
½ cup (3 oz) chopped candied orange peel

PLACE THE RAISINS in a small bowl and sprinkle with the sherry. Let stand for 1 hour, tossing occasionally.

IN THE BOWL OF A HEAVY-DUTY STAND MIXER, combine the flour, salt, sugar and yeast. In another bowl, using a fork or whisk, beat the eggs lightly, then mix in the warm milk, orange zest and vanilla. Stir the egg mixture into the flour mixture, mixing with a wooden spoon until a soft dough forms. Fit the mixer with the dough hook and knead on low speed until the dough is smooth and silky, about 15 minutes. Add the butter a few pieces at a time, mixing well after each addition until incorporated. Mix in the raisins and candied orange peel.

BUTTER A 2½-QUART KUGELHOPF OR BUNDT PAN. Transfer the dough to the pan, spreading it evenly and leveling the top with a rubber spatula. Cover the mold with buttered plastic wrap and let rise in a warm place until doubled in volume, about 1 hour.

PREHEAT AN OVEN to 350°F.

REMOVE THE PLASTIC WRAP and place the pan in the oven. Bake for 10 minutes, then reduce the heat to 325°F and continue to bake until golden brown, 45–50 minutes longer. Remove from the oven and let stand for 2–3 minutes, then unmold onto a wire rack and let cool. ✲

Honey Lemon Butter

This is excellent on crumpets, toast or slices of warm kugelhopf. Measure equal parts of unsalted butter and honey. Beat the butter until soft; slowly add the honey, beating until smooth. Stir in the grated zest of 1 lemon. Chill until the mixture is of spreading consistency.

GINGER,

in its various forms,
has always been a favorite
spice, but it wasn't until
around 1970 that ginger
in its crystallized form
became popular. Australian
crystallized ginger, made from
especially young and tender
roots, is considered to be
the best crystallized
ginger in the world. Ginger
tastes so delicious in desserts
and goes so well with orange
that it seemed natural to
combine the two flavors in
a steamed pudding. Serve
it with whipped cream
sweetened and flavored with
vanilla, rum or a
complementary liqueur.

GINGER-ORANGE STEAMED PUDDING

SERVES 8–10

3 cups (15 oz) all-purpose flour
2 tablespoons ground ginger
1¼ teaspoons baking soda
1 cup (6 oz) crystallized ginger, finely chopped
½ lb unsalted butter, at room temperature
1¼ cups (10 oz) sugar
5 eggs, lightly beaten
1 tablespoon brandy
finely grated zest of 1 orange
¼ cup (2 fl oz) fresh orange juice
boiling water, as needed
whipped cream flavored with vanilla extract or rum

GREASE A 2-QUART STEAMED PUDDING MOLD and its cover with butter. (If you do not have a pudding mold, use any deep mold or heatproof bowl and a cover of buttered aluminum foil secured with kitchen string.)

IN A BOWL, sift together the flour, ground ginger and baking soda. Stir in the crystallized ginger and set aside.

IN A LARGE BOWL, combine the butter and sugar. Using an electric mixer set on medium speed, beat until light and creamy, about 5 minutes. Add the eggs a little at a time, beating thoroughly after each addition. Then, beat until increased in volume slightly, 3–5 minutes. Beat in the brandy and the orange zest and juice. Add the flour mixture and beat just until smooth. Spoon the batter into the prepared pudding mold, avoiding air bubbles, and cover the mold.

PLACE THE MOLD on a trivet in a large pot and add boiling water to the pot to reach two-thirds up the mold sides. Cover the pot and simmer gently for 1½ hours. Add boiling water as needed to maintain original level.

REMOVE THE MOLD and let rest for 5 minutes. Invert onto a serving plate and lift off the mold. Serve warm or at room temperature, cut into wedges. Accompany with whipped cream. ✿

NUTMEG CUSTARD

SERVES 6

The great English cookery writer Elizabeth David first introduced me to the many ways you can use nutmeg, which I'd always thought of as a baking spice. She even wrote for us a little pamphlet, "The Nutmeg" (see right), which we gave out in the stores in 1975. Elizabeth also gave me this recipe, which allows the cook a lot of leeway in how much nutmeg is sprinkled over the individual custards during cooking, from the lightest dusting to a good coating. For the best nutmeg flavor, always grate it fresh, using a grater that includes a small compartment in which you can store a few whole nutmegs.

4 cups (32 fl oz) half-and-half
½ cup (4 oz) sugar
2 whole eggs, plus 6 egg yolks
2 teaspoons vanilla extract
freshly grated nutmeg

PREHEAT AN OVEN to 300°F.

IN A SAUCEPAN over medium heat, combine the half-and-half and sugar and heat, stirring, until the sugar dissolves and small bubbles appear around the edges of the pan. Remove from the heat.

IN A LARGE BOWL, whisk together the whole eggs and egg yolks until blended. Whisk a little of the hot milk mixture into the eggs, then slowly pour the remaining hot milk mixture into the eggs while whisking continuously. Whisk in the vanilla.

POUR THE EGG MIXTURE through a fine-mesh sieve into six 1-cup custard cups, dividing it evenly. Sprinkle the tops with a little nutmeg. Place the cups in a baking pan and pour boiling water into the pan to reach two-thirds up the sides of the cups. Cover the baking pan with aluminum foil.

BAKE UNTIL THE CUSTARDS ARE JUST SET and the tip of a knife inserted into the center of one comes out clean, about 1 hour. They should still tremble very slightly.

REMOVE THE BAKING PAN from the oven and let stand for a few minutes, then remove the custard cups and refrigerate until well chilled before serving. ♔

"It was a civilised fad, that 18th century love of portable nutmeg graters for the dining room, and the drawing room hot drinks, and for travelling. I see no reason why we shouldn't revive it. It is far from silly to carry a little nutmeg box and grater around in one's pocket. In London restaurants such a piece of equipment comes in handy. Here, even in Italian restaurants, I find it necessary to ask for nutmeg to grate on to my favourite plain pasta with butter and Parmesan, and for leaf spinach as well. To my mind nutmeg is essential to these dishes, as indeed it is to béchamel sauce, cheese soufflés, and nearly all other cheese mixtures."

—Elizabeth David

THE HISTORY OF TARTE TATIN

In the early years of the 20th century, rustic apple tarts were common around the small central French town of Lamotte-Beuvron, on the road between Paris and Toulouse. The best of them, however, was made by two sisters, Caroline and Stephanie Tatin, who ran an inn near the railway station. So spectacular was their version that even Curnonsky, the renowned epicurean and champion of regional French cooking, ventured from Paris to try it. Soon the carmelized apple tart became forever linked with the Tatin sisters.

TARTE TATIN

MAKES ONE 9-INCH TART; SERVES 8

For a time in the mid-1970s, tarte Tatin was the must-have dessert on chic restaurant menus. The classic French upside-down caramelized apple tart has gone on to become a favorite in this country, and justly so. The owner of Matfer, the French bakeware manufacturer, once took me to a small restaurant near his factory on the outskirts of Paris where I had the best tarte Tatin I've ever tasted. I have tried many times since to duplicate it. This one comes close.

FOR THE PASTRY:
1¼ cups (6½ oz) all-purpose flour
¼ teaspoon salt
1 tablespoon sugar
½ cup (4 oz) unsalted butter, chilled, cut into small cubes
1–2 tablespoons ice water

FOR THE FILLING:
⅓ cup (3 oz) unsalted butter, at room temperature, plus
  2 tablespoons unsalted butter, melted
1 cup (8 oz) sugar
4 lb Golden Delicious apples

TO MAKE THE PASTRY, in a bowl, stir together the flour, salt and sugar. Add the butter and, using a pastry blender or fingers, quickly cut the butter into the flour until crumbly and the mixture resembles oatmeal. Then, while quickly stirring and tossing with a fork, add the ice water a little at a time just until the dough forms a loose ball. Gather into a ball, wrap in plastic wrap and refrigerate for 30 minutes.

TO MAKE THE FILLING, spread the ⅓ cup softened butter on the bottom and sides of an ovenproof frying pan 9 inches in diameter and 2 inches deep. Sprinkle ¾ cup of the sugar over the butter.

PEEL, QUARTER AND CORE THE APPLES and cut each quarter into 3 wedges. Place the wedges in a large bowl. Drizzle the 2 tablespoons melted butter over the apples and toss to coat evenly. Form a layer of the apple wedges in the bottom of the prepared pan, arranging them in overlapping concentric circles and packing them closely together. Continue arranging the remaining apple wedges in layers, packing them tightly. Sprinkle the remaining ¼ cup sugar evenly over the apples. Place over medium-high heat and cook until a thick syrup forms and is bubbling up and the apples are partially cooked, 8–10 minutes, adjusting the heat to keep them from burning. Remove from the heat and set aside to cool a little, about 20 minutes.

PREHEAT AN OVEN to 425°F. Place the dough on a lightly floured work surface and flatten into a round cake with your hands. Dust with flour and roll out into a round a little larger than the diameter of the frying pan. Carefully transfer the dough round to the pan, draping it over the apples to cover them completely and tucking the edges inside the pan. Place the pan on a rimmed baking sheet.

BAKE UNTIL THE PASTRY IS NICELY BROWNED, the apples are tender and the juices are thick, 30–40 mintues. Remove from the oven and place over high heat. Cook, shaking the pan to loosen the apples on the bottom, for another 6–7 minutes to evaporate any juices and to caramelize the sugar. Remove from the heat and set aside to cool for 10–12 minutes.

TO SERVE, invert a serving plate over the pan. Holding the plate and pan together, turn them over so the tart falls onto the plate. Lift off the pan and serve the tart warm. ♛

Hot Fruit Compote

Country fruit desserts can be extraordinarily simple and delicious, as our ever-deepening knowledge of French country cooking has taught us.

I like to serve this dessert in winter, when simple food is especially welcome after the excesses of the holiday season. I bake and serve it in a shallow, white fluted dish, erroneously termed a quiche dish, which of course it is not— pastry does not brown well in porcelain.

Assemble a combination of peeled and quartered bananas, pears, and pitted prunes (soak the prunes in red wine over-night). Purée a handful of fresh or frozen raspberries and add the juice of 2 or 3 oranges and about 3 tablespoons honey. Stir well and pour over the fruit. This adds color as well as an extra fruity flavor. Bake at 350°F until bubbling, 15–20 minutes. Just before serving, grate the zest of 1 lime over the top.

SOUFFLE AU PAMPLEMOUSSE

SERVES 6

I was given this soufflé recipe by the chef at Chez Lucienne, a restaurant on the Left Bank in Paris in the early 1960s.

6 large grapefruits
1 cup (5 oz) all-purpose flour
½ cup (4 oz) granulated sugar
½ cup (4 fl oz) heavy cream
½ cup (4 fl oz) milk
5 egg yolks, plus 6 egg whites
1 tablespoon kirsch, or more to taste
confectioners' sugar

USING A SHARP KNIFE, cut off about one-fourth of each grapefruit from the stem end in an even slice. Working with 1 grapefruit at a time, hold the grapefruits over a bowl and, using a spoon, scrape out all the pulp, including the membrane, from each one, letting it drop into the bowl. Pour the contents of the bowl into a fine-mesh sieve placed over another bowl and press on the pulp with the back of a large spoon, forcing out as much juice as possible. Measure out 1 cup juice; reserve the remainder for another use. Place the grapefruit shells on a baking sheet.

PREHEAT AN OVEN to 375°F. In a bowl, combine the flour, granulated sugar, cream, milk and the 1 cup grapefruit juice and stir until smooth. Add the egg yolks one at a time, beating until fully incorporated after each addition. Add the kirsch and stir well. In another bowl, using a whisk or electric mixer, beat the egg whites until stiff peaks form. Using a rubber spatula, stir about one-fourth of the egg whites into the yolk mixture to lighten it, then gently fold in the remaining whites just until no white streaks remain; do not overmix.

SPOON THE MIXTURE into the grapefruit shells, filling to within ½ inch of the tops. Bake until the tops have risen and are lightly browned, about 20 minutes. Remove from the oven. Using a sifter or fine-mesh sieve, sift confectioners' sugar over the tops, then serve immediately. ✲

ZABAGLIONE

SERVES 4–6

There were many Italian restaurants in San Francisco in the 1970s where zabaglione, the frothy dessert of beaten egg yolks, sugar and Marsala, was served. Eating it was a memorable experience that many diners tried to duplicate at home, and most found it easy to make.

4 egg yolks
¼ cup (2 oz) sugar
½ cup (4 fl oz) sweet Marsala wine

IN A MEDIUM-SIZED HEATPROOF BOWL or the top pan of a double boiler, combine the egg yolks and sugar. Using a whisk, beat until light colored and creamy, 2–3 minutes. Add the Marsala and whisk until well blended. Place the bowl or pan over (not touching) simmering water in a saucepan or the bottom pan of the double boiler. Whisk continuously until the mixture has tripled in volume and is quite thick and creamy; the top should stand in thick folds. This will take 10–15 minutes. Be careful that the mixture does not get too hot or the eggs will curdle.

SPOON INTO STEMMED GLASSES and serve at once. ✲

An unlined copper zabaglione pot makes whipping up a batch of the quick-to-assemble dessert even easier. The pan's rounded bottom allows for uniform, thorough whisking, while its long handle lets you hold it over a flame or simmering water. The top pan of a double boiler or any pan that you can hold over simmering water will also work well, however, just as long as you are careful to whisk the mixture evenly and thoroughly so none of it adheres to the pan sides.

The Perfect Cup of Tea

Tea connoisseurs insist that the best way to make tea is in a china teapot using freshly drawn cold water that has been brought to a rapid boil. Rinse the pot with boiling water, and add a teaspoon of tea leaves for each cup. Add the boiling water, let steep for 3–5 minutes and stir to insure uniform flavor. Serve with a choice of lemon, milk and sugar, but not cream, which overpowers, instead of enhances, the taste.

WALNUT LACE COOKIES

MAKES ABOUT 5 DOZEN COOKIES

Sometime in the mid 1960s, Helen White, the manager of the Francisca Club, right across from Williams-Sonoma's Sutter Street store in San Francisco, sketched out this recipe for the club's wonderfully thin, crisp cookies. You really do need to line the baking sheet with parchment paper, or you'll have a devil of a time trying to remove the cookies.

2 tablespoons all-purpose flour
½ teaspoon baking soda
½ teaspoon salt
½ cup (4 oz) unsalted butter, at room temperature, cut into small cubes
1 cup (8 oz) sugar
2 eggs, lightly beaten
1 teaspoon vanilla extract
1½ cups (6 oz) walnuts, coarsely chopped

PREHEAT AN OVEN to 375°F. Line a baking sheet with parchment paper.

IN A SMALL BOWL, sift together the flour, baking soda and salt. In another bowl, combine the butter and sugar. Using an electric mixer set on medium speed, beat until light and creamy, about 5 minutes. Add the eggs and vanilla and beat until smooth. Using a rubber spatula, fold the flour mixture into the butter mixture, then stir in the walnuts.

USING A TEASPOON, place small mounds of the batter 4 inches apart on the prepared baking sheet. (They will spread during baking.) Bake until evenly browned, 10–12 minutes. Remove from the oven and slide the parchment paper off of the baking sheet onto a work surface. Let cool until the cookies have hardened, 1–2 minutes. Using a flat spatula, transfer the cookies to a wire rack to cool completely. Wipe off the parchment with a paper towel and repeat with the remaining batter. Store the cooled cookies in an airtight tin for up to 2 weeks. ♖

TOMATO PRESERVES

MAKES ABOUT 5 CUPS

Before and after World War II, a dessert you would probably encounter in a Paris pension was tomato preserves and fromage blanc.

5 cups (2½ lb) sugar
1 cup water
2½–2¾ lb ripe, juicy tomatoes, peeled, seeded (see page 70) and
  diced (4 cups)
1 piece vanilla bean, 4 inches long, split halfway through lengthwise to expose the seeds

IN A HEAVY SAUCEPAN over high heat, combine the sugar and water. Bring to a boil, stirring to dissolve the sugar. Add the tomatoes, adjust the heat to maintain a gentle boil and boil steadily for 30 minutes, stirring frequently. Add the vanilla bean and continue boiling until the jelling stage is reached, 15–20 minutes longer. To test, remove from the heat. Fill a chilled spoon with the preserves, then slowly pour the preserves back into the pan; the last two drops should merge and fall from the spoon in a sheet. Alternatively, test with a candy thermometer; it should register 220°–222°F. Using a large spoon, skim off any foam from the surface.

MEANWHILE, wash canning jars and lids in hot soapy water and rinse well in clear hot water. Fill the jars with hot water. Place the lids in a small saucepan, add water to cover and bring to a simmer over high heat. Remove from the heat.

DRAIN 1 JAR. Spoon the hot preserves into the jar to within ¼ inch of the top. Using a hot damp towel, wipe the rim clean, then remove a lid from the saucepan and cover the jar. Seal with a screw band. Repeat with the remaining preserves and jars.

PLACE THE FILLED JARS (not touching) on a metal rack in a large pot and add boiling water to cover by at least 1 inch. Cover, bring to a boil and boil for 10 minutes. Remove the jars from the water bath and let stand at room temperature until cool, then check for seal. The lids should have a slight depression in the center. Store in a cool, dry place for up to 1 year; once opened, store in the refrigerator for up to 2 weeks. If a proper seal has not formed, refrigerate for up to 2 weeks. ❧

Coeur à la Crème with Tomato Preserves

To make this light-textured after-dinner cheese, force 1 lb each of cottage cheese and cream cheese through a fine-mesh sieve placed over a bowl. Stir in 2 cups (16 fl oz) heavy cream, blending well, and season lightly with salt. Line a heart-shaped mold with cheesecloth, and pack with the cheese mixture. Stand the mold on a plate in the refrigerator overnight to drain off the petit lait (whey). Unmold onto a flat platter and remove the cheesecloth. Serve with tomato preserves.

Poached Pears with Tomato Preserves

To make this refreshingly different dessert, first make a simple syrup: Combine 4 cups (2 lb) sugar with 4 cups water in a wide, shallow pan. Bring to a boil, stirring to dissolve the sugar, and add the juice of ½ lemon. Peel 4 firm, ripe Bartlett pears, cut in half lengthwise, and enlarge the central cavity with a melon baller, removing the core at the same time. Add the pears to the simmering syrup and poach until tender, about 20 minutes. Remove, drain and let cool. Just before serving, fill the centers with tomato preserves.

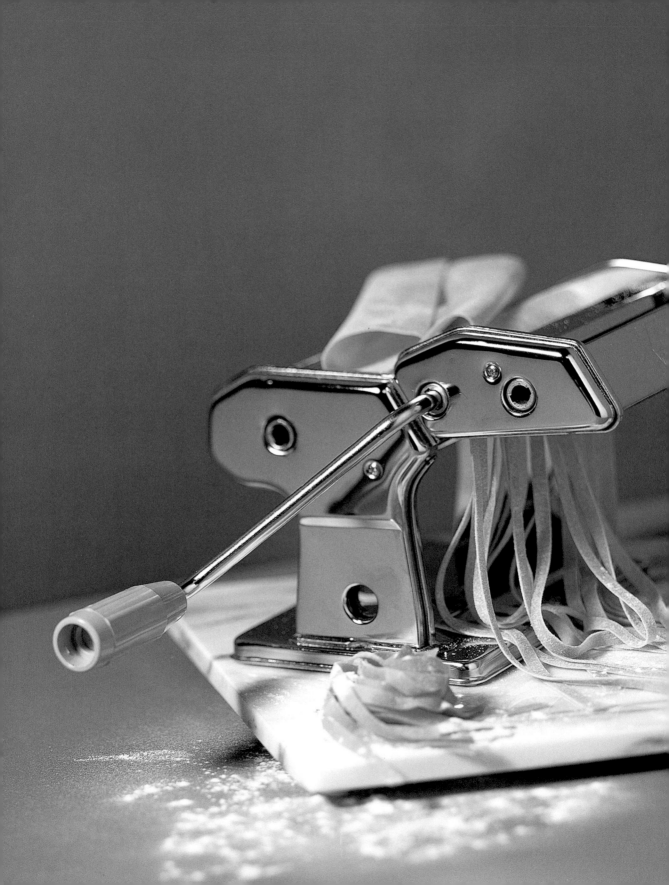

1976–1986
BECOMING SERIOUS COOKS

During Williams-Sonoma's third decade, I saw our customers not just taking pleasure in cooking but actually dedicating themselves to becoming serious cooks. A few trends from those years—especially the arrival of some exciting new kitchen equipment and the growth of interest in Italian cooking—will give you a good idea of what I mean.

Look at the food processor, for example. Carl Sontheimer, a brilliant engineer who even invented some of the devices on the first lunar lander, discovered a French professional chefs' kitchen machine called the Robot-Coupe. As a retirement pastime, he acquired the rights to import the machine to the United States in the early 1970s, which he did under a name he originated, Cuisinart. Although he introduced it here as early as 1973, the Cuisinart food processor didn't really take off until the late 1970s, when home cooks finally discovered how quickly, easily and neatly the machine could slice, chop and purée large quantities of ingredients, mix batters and bread doughs, and perform all kinds of other tasks. Half a million machines sold in 1977 alone.

The same people who were buying food processors in such great numbers were also hungry for books and magazines that could teach them how to be better cooks.

The same people who were buying food processors in such great numbers were also hungry for books and magazines that could teach them how to be better cooks. Richard Olney, who wrote two of the best French cookbooks of the early 1970s, shared his in-depth knowledge of classic techniques in Time-Life's step-by-step cooking series, The Good Cook, which began publication in the late 1970s. French chef Jacques Pépin did likewise, establishing for himself a nationwide reputation through his books *La Technique* (1976) and *La Méthode* (1979) that continues to this day. And while we still read *Gourmet,* a newcomer called *Bon Appétit* became the most-talked-about food magazine, growing in monthly circulation from 240,000 copies in 1976 to 1.3 million copies by 1981.

You might be surprised to learn that a term we all now take for granted was coined during these years, too. In August 1982, the British magazine *Harpers & Queen* first referred to people serious about good cooking and fine dining as "foodies."

But we weren't only indulging in French cooking. Another piece of kitchen equipment which excited people was the pasta machine. This reflected the popularity of fresh pasta specifically and Italian regional cooking in general during the late 1970s and early 1980s, a trend I saw driven by the widespread growth of good Italian restaurants, delicatessens and fresh pasta shops and by such books as *The Classic Italian Cook Book* (1973) by Marcella Hazan, *Mediterranean Cooking* (1977) by Paula Wolfert and *The Cuisine of Venice & Surrounding Northern Regions* (1978) by Hedy Giusti-Lanham

and Andrea Dodi. Thousands of hand-cranked Atlas pasta machines and electric pasta makers were sold to home cooks who discovered how good freshly made pasta could be and how easy it was to pre-pare. In 1982, *People* magazine even ran a picture of me in my kitchen tossing a bunch of fresh fettuccine I'd just made!

In the late 1970s, Williams-Sonoma also played a part in the growing craze for *aceto balsamico,* Italian balsamic vinegar, which we began to import around 1978 exclusively from Fini, the landmark company in Modena. Those years, too, saw the first great surge of interest in olive oil, with serious cooks learning the significance of the word *extra-virgin* and com-paring the colors, aromas and flavors of oils from different Italian, as well as other Mediterranean and Californian, suppliers. In the early 1980s we imported our first extra-virgin olive oil from the Tuscan farm of the Olivieri family, whose daughter, Maria Olivieri Quinn, lived in San Francisco. Another popular oil came from Badia a Coltibuono, the Tuscan estate of Lorenza de' Medici, who, by the end of the 1980s, had herself earned a solid reputation in America as an Italian cooking expert.

Olive oils and vinegars weren't the only food products I brought back from my buying trips to Italy in those years. In San Francisco in the early 1980s, we opened the first American branch of Il Fornaio, the high-quality Italian bakery chain that I discovered in Florence. It played a big part in introducing serious cooks and eaters to the plea-sures of authentic Italian bread. I convinced the Il Fornaio bakers to give me recipes for some of their best loaves. I adapted and tested those recipes for the home oven and then put them in our catalog.

Sharing their discoveries was important to serious cooks. For evi-dence of this, you don't have to look any further than *Entertaining,* a best-selling book published in 1982 that introduced us to an ingenious woman named Martha Stewart. Her books, along with those of such authors as Lee Bailey, Christopher Idone and the *Silver Palate* team of Julee Rosso and Sheila Lukins, showed us how cooking becomes all the more pleasurable when it is shared with others.

Before the 1980s, you would be lucky if you could find one brand of olive oil on your local food store's shelves. Today, finely made olive oils from small producers in California and the Mediterranean give us a wide variety from which to choose.

Sauteed Mushrooms

SERVES 4–6

This recipe for a passed hors d'oeuvre of quickly sautéed mushrooms grew out of my desire to show what one could do with a proper French-style sauté pan. Look for a heavy metal pan (such as very thick aluminum) that is wide enough to accommodate a generous quantity of mushrooms in a single layer. Such a pan holds and transfers heat well, to ensure that the mushrooms brown without becoming soggy. You can serve the mushrooms with toothpicks, as the recipe suggests, or place them on slices from a French baguette to make canapés.

1 lb small fresh mushrooms
3–4 tablespoons unsalted butter
½ lemon
salt and freshly ground pepper
chopped fresh parsley

CLEAN THE MUSHROOMS by brushing off any dirt with a dry towel or mushroom brush.

IN A SAUTÉ PAN over medium-high heat, melt 3 tablespoons of the butter. When hot, add the mushrooms and sauté, stirring and tossing constantly, for 1–2 minutes. Squeeze in a few drops of lemon juice and season to taste with salt, pepper and parsley. Continue to sauté, stirring and tossing, until just tender, 1–2 minutes longer, adding more butter if necessary. Do not overcook; they should be a velvety light beige.

TRANSFER TO A WARMED SERVING PLATE and serve at once with toothpicks for spearing. ✾

LENTIL SOUP

SERVES 4–6

When I was a kid, lentils had a reputation of being something poor people ate. Only in the mid-1970s, with the rise of interest in Italian cooking, did Americans learn how good this ingredient could be. The use of tomatoes, oregano and olive oil in this soup is typically Italian, and there is nothing poor about the way it tastes.

2 cups (14 oz) dried lentils
6 cups water
2 teaspoons salt, plus salt to taste
1 yellow onion stuck with 2 whole cloves, plus 2 yellow onions,
  chopped
1 bay leaf
2 fresh oregano sprigs or 1 teaspoon dried oregano
3 tablespoons olive oil
3 lb ripe plum tomatoes, peeled, seeded (see page 70) and chopped
4 cups (32 fl oz) chicken stock, or as needed
freshly ground pepper
chopped fresh parsley

SORT THROUGH THE LENTILS, discarding any discolored ones or impurities. Rinse, drain and place in a large saucepan with the water. Place over medium-high heat and add the 2 teaspoons salt, the clove-studded onion, bay leaf and oregano. Bring just to a boil, reduce the heat to medium-low, cover partially and simmer until the lentils are just tender, about 30 minutes. Drain and discard the onion and cloves, bay leaf and the oregano sprigs, if using. Set the lentils aside.

IN A LARGE SAUCEPAN over medium-low heat, warm the olive oil. When hot, add the chopped onions and sauté gently, stirring, until translucent, 3–5 minutes. Add the tomatoes and cook gently, uncovered, until the tomatoes break down and the juices are released, 10–15 minutes longer.

STIR in the 4 cups stock and the reserved lentils, cover partially and simmer gently over medium-low heat until the flavors are well blended, 10–15 minutes longer. Add more stock or water if the soup seems too thick. Season to taste with salt and pepper.

TO SERVE, ladle into warmed bowls and sprinkle with parsley. ❦

While you find lentils in varying shades of tan, brown and orange, I especially like the green Puy lentil, named for the area in which it is grown around Le Puy in the Auvergne region of France. Green lentils are also now being cultivated in the United States. You'll find them in specialty-food stores and in the international-food sections of large markets.

"Julia Child, James Beard and Craig Claiborne have all agreed—the Cuisinart Food Processor is the greatest French invention for years. It makes faultless pastry in 20 seconds, classic mayonnaise in 45, chops beef in 10. . . . This machine does a great deal more than a blender can . . . It shreds, slices, chops and grinds (marvelous for coleslaw, French onion soup and pâtés) . . . Pastry forms itself into a neat convoluted roll before your astonished eyes; in fact, it's an effort of will not to stand there feeding the machine flour, butter and ice-water all morning! In short, the French have done it again."

—Williams-Sonoma, "A Catalog for Cooks" (1976)

CARROT SOUP WITH CORIANDER

SERVES 6

The arrival of the food processor in the late 1970s revolutionized the way Americans were making soups. We discovered the puréed soup, which could be assembled from all sorts of different vegetables, like the carrots used here. This recipe shows how we were becoming more adventurous with our use of exotic spices and fresh herbs. The ground coriander and chopped cilantro give the soup its wonderfully bright, fresh taste.

⅓ cup (3 oz) unsalted butter
1 small yellow onion, diced
1 tablespoon chopped garlic
2 lb carrots (12–14), peeled and cut crosswise into slices
  ½ inch thick
1 baking potato, 8–9 oz, peeled and cut into small cubes
1 teaspoon ground coriander
4 cups (32 fl oz) chicken stock
½ teaspoon sugar
¼ teaspoon salt
2 cups (16 fl oz) milk, or as needed
freshly ground pepper
2–3 tablespoons dry sherry

½ cup (4 fl oz) sour cream
¼ cup chopped fresh cilantro

IN A LARGE SAUCEPAN over medium-low heat, melt the butter. When hot, add the onion and sauté, stirring occasionally, until translucent, 3–5 minutes. Add the garlic and sauté, stirring, until beginning to change color, 20–30 seconds. Add the carrots, potato and ground coriander and sauté, stirring a couple of times, for 2–3 minutes. Add the stock, sugar and salt and raise the heat to medium. Bring to a simmer, reduce the heat to medium-low, cover partially and continue simmering until the vegetables are soft when pierced with the tip of a knife, 20–25 minutes. Remove from the heat.

IN A FOOD PROCESSOR fitted with the metal blade or in a blender, process the vegetables in small batches with their stock until smooth (the soup may be made ahead to this point, covered and refrigerated for up to 2 days).

RETURN THE PURÉE to the saucepan and add 2 cups (16 fl oz) milk and pepper to taste. Place over medium heat and heat almost to a boil. Taste and adjust the seasonings. If the soup is too thick, add milk as needed to thin. Just before serving, stir in the sherry to taste.

TO SERVE, ladle into warmed soup bowls. Top each bowl with a spoonful of sour cream and a sprinkling of cilantro. Serve at once. ✿

WALNUT OIL

In the early 1980s, there was a burst of interest in walnut oil, which adds a rich flavor to this dressing. Look for toasted walnut oil. It can turn rancid in a short time, however, so buy it in small quantities from a store that has a good turn-over, and store it in an airtight container in a cool place away from light.

MEDITERRANEAN SALAD

SERVES 4–6

½ cup (2 oz) walnuts
2 tablespoons white wine vinegar
⅛ teaspoon salt
freshly ground pepper
5 tablespoons (2½ fl oz) toasted walnut oil
3 tablespoons mild vegetable oil such as safflower oil
2 heads Bibb lettuce
1 cup (6 oz) seedless white grapes, rinsed, dried and cut in half
½ cup (2½ oz) crumbled feta cheese, preferably made from sheep's milk

PREHEAT AN OVEN to 350°F. Spread the walnuts on a baking sheet and toast until they begin to color and are fragrant, 5–10 minutes. Remove from the oven and set aside to cool.

IN A SMALL BOWL, combine the vinegar, salt and pepper to taste and stir until the salt dissolves. Add the walnut oil and vegetable oil and whisk until well blended. Set aside.

DISCARD ANY TOUGH or discolored outer leaves from the lettuce heads. Rinse and thoroughly dry the remaining leaves, then tear into bite-sized pieces. Place in a large salad bowl. Break or cut the walnuts into small pieces and scatter over the lettuce. Scatter the grapes and cheese over the lettuce. Whisk the dressing again and drizzle over the salad. Toss well and serve immediately on individual plates. 🖤

BLACKSMITH SALAD

SERVES 6

On my buying trips to Italy in the late 1970s, I always went into the sixth-floor food department of the Renascente department store in Milan to see what was new. I kept noticing small frosted bottles that were labeled aceto balsamico, *from a company called Fini. Not knowing Italian, for all I knew it could have been hair tonic. Finally, I found out that it was a special "balsamic vinegar" made in Modena for centuries. I tasted it and it was fabulous, unlike any vinegar I had ever tried. Williams-Sonoma started importing it exclusively from Fini around 1978, making us one of the first to make* aceto balsamico *available in America. The people at Fini gave me the recipe for this rustic Italian salad, which shows off good balsamic vinegar in the simplest of ways. Usually, Italian waiters do not mix the oil and vinegar together before tossing them with the salad. Instead, they toss the salad with the vinegar and then with the oil, believing that this order keeps the vinegar from falling to the bottom of the bowl.*

1 large or 2 small heads butter lettuce
1 piece Parmesan cheese, 3 oz
2 tablespoons balsamic vinegar
pinch of salt
⅓ cup (3 fl oz) extra-virgin olive oil

CHILL THE SALAD BOWL, but do not allow it to become too cold or the lettuce leaves will stick to it.

DISCARD ANY TOUGH or discolored outer leaves from the lettuce head(s). Separate, rinse and thoroughly dry the remaining leaves, then tear any large leaves into pieces. Place in the chilled salad bowl. Using a vegetable peeler, slice the Parmesan cheese into very thin chips and scatter them over the lettuce. Sprinkle with the vinegar and salt, and toss well. Drizzle the oil over the top and toss again. Serve immediately on individual plates. 🖤

ACETO BALSAMICO

This legendary Italian wine vinegar has been made in Modena in the same way for countless generations. Ideally, the maturing vinegar is carefully transferred to kegs of decreasing size and of different woods (juniper, mulberry, oak, and chestnut) which are left slightly open to breathe over a 25-year aging period before bottling. The vinegar grows deeper and more intense in color and flavor with each decanting. The result is a condiment of amazing subtlety and richness. Add a few drops to a salad dressing, to broiled meats, even to fresh strawberries. Place a spoonful into the cavity of avocado halves for a delicious salad.

"Young French chef Michel Guérard has scandalized the world of haute cuisine with his new concept of preparing marvelous French food without the calories. *Time* magazine put him on their cover last February and hailed it as "The Cuisine of Slimness." The battle cry of the late, great Chef Fernand Point was *Du beurre! Donnes-moi du beurre! Toujours du beurre!* (Butter! Give me butter! Always butter!) Michel Guérard doesn't agree, and to prove his point has documented his views in a thoroughly original cookery book, Michel Guérard's *Cuisine Minceur* . . . We suspect that *la cuisine minceur* is here to stay."

—Williams-Sonoma, "A Catalog for Cooks" (1977)

MARSEILLES FISH STEW

SERVES 4–6

I find it interesting how Americans were often introduced to French cooking through its more complicated dishes and then, as our knowledge grew, we found simpler but no less authentic ways to arrive at similar effects. This stew is a good example. Although related to bouillabaisse, the legendary southern French seafood stew, this culinary cousin is much easier to make, starting with the fact that you don't need a fish stock. Yet, it draws considerable flavor from the saffron, paprika, garlic, onion, leek, tomatoes and fresh herbs.

1 leek
½ teaspoon saffron threads
pinch of salt, plus salt to taste
3 tablespoons olive oil
3 cloves garlic, minced
1 yellow onion, chopped
¼ teaspoon hot paprika
1 celery stalk, diced
1 carrot, peeled and diced
3 baking potatoes, peeled and cubed
3 ripe tomatoes, peeled (see page 70) and quartered

1 bay leaf
2 fresh thyme sprigs
3 fresh parsley sprigs
2 orange zest strips, each 3 inches long and 1 inch wide
2 cups water
1 cup (8 fl oz) dry white wine
freshly ground pepper
2½ lb assorted white fish fillets such as sole, halibut, sea bass
  and/or snapper in any combination

TRIM THE LEEK, leaving about 1 inch of the tender green top intact. Remove and discard any old leaves. Make a lengthwise slit along the leek to within about 2 inches of the root end. Hold the leek under cold running water and separate the leaves slightly to rinse away any dirt lodged between the layers. Slice and set aside.

PLACE THE SAFFRON and the pinch of salt in a large metal spoon. Hold the spoon over a hot stove-top burner for a few seconds, then, using the back of a teaspoon, crush the saffron threads into a powder. Set aside.

IN A SAUCEPAN over medium-low heat, warm the olive oil. When hot, add the garlic, onion, leek and paprika and sauté gently, stirring constantly, until the onion is translucent, 3–5 minutes. Add the celery, carrot, potatoes and tomatoes and cook, stirring occasionally, for another 5 minutes.

GATHER TOGETHER the bay leaf, thyme, parsley and orange zest into a bouquet and tie securely with kitchen string. Add to the saucepan along with the powdered saffron, water, wine and salt and pepper to taste. Bring to a simmer over medium heat, cover and continue to simmer until the vegetables are just tender, 15–20 minutes.

CUT THE FISH FILLETS into medium-sized pieces and add them to the pan, carefully submerging them in the juices. Cover and simmer gently over medium-low heat until the fish is opaque throughout when pierced with a knife, 10–15 minutes.

REMOVE AND DISCARD the herb bouquet. Taste and adjust the seasonings. Ladle into warmed soup plates and serve immediately. ✦

Sea Bass with Dried Fennel

Our growing appreciation of Mediterranean cooking during this era joined with the all-American love of outdoor grilling to popularize this innovative, easy way to flavor seafood cooked in the open air.

During the last few minutes of grilling a whole sea bass (or fillets) over a charcoal or wood-chip fire, place a few stalks of dried fennel on the coals and let them flame up. Turn the fish once.

If using a hinged, footed basket grill, after cooking the fish over a charcoal or wood-chip fire, place the fish, still in the basket, over a fireproof dish containing a few stalks of dried fennel that have been sprinkled with Cognac. Ignite and flame the fish.

CLAMS ALGARVE

SERVES 4–6

I started visiting Portugal in the late 1970s. My agent there once took me to a restaurant north of Lisbon that specialized in seafood dishes from the province of Algarve in southern Portugal. The waiter brought to the table a cataplana, *a hinged copper cooking vessel shaped like a clamshell, and nested it on a towel rolled into a ring. When he opened the pan, out came billows of steam with the marvelous aromas of white fish fillets steamed on a bed of bitter greens resembling Swiss chard. Later, I discovered this traditional, easy way to cook clams in a* cataplana. *A heavy saucepan will also work well. This is delicious served with crusty French bread.*

3 lb small clams, well scrubbed
2 tablespoons olive oil
2 yellow onions, thinly sliced
dash of hot-pepper sauce such as Tabasco
salt and freshly ground pepper
2–3 oz smoked ham, cut into matchstick strips
2–3 oz chorizo, thinly sliced
1 cup (8 fl oz) dry white wine
1 tablespoon chopped fresh parsley

DISCARD ANY OPEN CLAMS that do not close to the touch. Set aside.

IN A HEAVY SAUCEPAN over medium-low heat, warm the olive oil. When hot, add the onions, hot-pepper sauce and salt and pepper to taste and sauté until the onions are translucent, 7–10 minutes. Do not allow to brown.

ADD THE HAM, chorizo and wine. Cover, reduce the heat to low and cook gently for about 15 minutes to blend the flavors. Raise the heat to medium-high, add the clams and scatter the parsley over the clams. Cover tightly and cook, shaking the pan occasionally and tossing the clams once or twice, until the clams open, about 5 minutes. Discard any clams that did not open. Using a slotted spoon, transfer the clams to warmed soup plates or bowls. Spoon the broth, together with the ham and sausage, over the top. Serve immediately.

Baked Fruits de Mer

Here's a classic French seafood recipe that offers the simplicity and good taste we all seek in our busy lives.

Place 2 or 3 each scallops, shrimp and cooked crab meat pieces in shell dishes or ramekins. Sprinkle with chopped shallots, parsley and tarragon. Season with salt and freshly ground pepper. Dribble a good olive oil and a little dry vermouth over the top. Bake in a 400°F oven until cooked through, about 10 minutes. Serve immediately with French bread.

SOLE FILLETS WITH DILL

SERVES 4

In this decade, fresh dill was one of the many herbs being planted in backyards or window boxes, or it was easily found in local food stores or produce shops. This simple dish takes just minutes to prepare.

6 tablespoons (3 oz) unsalted butter, melted
2 tablespoons finely chopped yellow onion
2 tablespoons finely chopped celery
1 cup (2 oz) fresh bread crumbs
2 teaspoons chopped fresh dill or 1 teaspoon dried dill
juice of ½ lemon
pinch of salt
4 sole fillets, 6–8 oz each
chopped fresh parsley

PREHEAT AN OVEN to 400°F. Butter a shallow 2-quart baking dish.

PLACE 1 TABLESPOON of the butter in a sauté pan or frying pan over medium-low heat. When hot, add the onion and celery and sauté, stirring, until translucent, about 3 minutes. Stir in the bread crumbs, dill, lemon juice and salt. Set aside.

PLACE THE SOLE FILLETS in the prepared baking dish in a single layer. Cover evenly with the bread crumb mixture and drizzle with the remaining butter. Bake until the fish is opaque throughout when pierced with a knife and the top is lightly browned, 8–10 minutes. If the top has not browned, slip into a preheated broiler about 4 inches from the heat and broil briefly to brown the crumbs lightly. Sprinkle with parsley and serve at once directly from the baking dish.

POT ROAST OF BEEF WITH ACETO BALSAMICO

SERVES 8–10

As balsamic vinegar became more and more popular, I enjoyed finding original ways to use it. Serve this over potatoes or noodles to soak up all the fragrant juices.

¼ cup (2 fl oz) olive oil
1 piece beef rump, chuck or round, 4–5 lb
1 yellow onion, sliced
1 carrot, peeled and sliced
1 celery stalk, sliced
1 bay leaf
3 whole cloves
3 fresh thyme sprigs or 1 teaspoon dried thyme
3 fresh parsley sprigs
2 tablespoons balsamic vinegar
1 cup water
salt and freshly ground pepper

IN A LARGE, HEAVY POT over medium-high heat, warm the olive oil. When hot, add the meat and brown well on all sides, 8–10 minutes. Transfer to a plate.

REDUCE THE HEAT to medium and add the onion, carrot and celery. Sauté, stirring, until the onion is translucent, 5–7 minutes. Add the bay leaf, cloves, thyme and parsley. Return the meat to the pot, sprinkle with the vinegar and add the water. Reduce the heat to low, cover and cook at a very gentle simmer for 2 hours, turning once halfway through the cooking. Season with salt and pepper to taste, re-cover and cook until tender when pierced with a fork, about 30 minutes longer.

REMOVE FROM THE HEAT and let rest in the pot, covered, for 5 minutes. Transfer the meat to a warmed platter. Tent loosely with aluminum foil to keep warm. Strain the pot juices through a fine-mesh sieve into a saucepan and skim off the fat with a large spoon. Place over high heat and boil until reduced by half, 3–5 minutes. Taste and adjust the seasonings.

CARVE THE POT ROAST. Pour the reduced juices into a warmed bowl and serve alongside. ❧

Carrots with Aceto Balsamico

Here's another use for balsamic vinegar: Peel and thinly slice 5 or 6 carrots. Place in a saucepan with ¼ cup water, 1 tablespoon unsalted butter and a little salt. Cover tightly and simmer over low heat until the carrots are just tender, 15–20 minutes. The carrots will have absorbed the water; if they have not, uncover and cook briefly to evaporate any remaining water; watch carefully so they do not burn. In a separate saucepan over medium-low heat, combine 3 tablespoons brown sugar, 2 tablespoons unsalted butter and 1 teaspoon balsamic vinegar and cook, stirring, until well blended, 1–2 minutes. Pour over the carrots, toss and serve.

FRENCH VEAL CASSEROLE

SERVES 8–10

½ cup (4 oz) unsalted butter, at room temperature
3 lb boneless veal shoulder, trimmed of fat and cut
  into 1½-inch cubes
2 large yellow onions, chopped
1 clove garlic, minced
6 carrots, peeled and cut on the diagonal into large ovals
2 cups (16 fl oz) chicken stock
1 bay leaf
1 tablespoon finely chopped fresh parsley
1 teaspoon dried oregano
salt and freshly ground pepper
3 tablespoons all-purpose flour
10–12 oz fresh button mushrooms, wiped clean
½ cup (4 fl oz) heavy cream

PREHEAT AN OVEN to 350°F. In a sauté pan over medium-high heat, melt 2 tablespoons of the butter. When hot, add the veal cubes in batches and lightly brown on all sides, 5–6 minutes, adding more butter if needed. Transfer to a deep 3-quart baking dish with a cover or a Dutch oven. Reduce the heat to medium, add the onions and garlic to the same sauté pan and sauté, adding more butter if needed, until golden, 6–8 minutes, adding the carrots during the last few minutes. Add the stock, bay leaf, parsley, oregano and salt and pepper to taste and stir well. In a small bowl, mix together the flour and a little of the remaining butter to form a smooth paste and add to the sauté pan. Stir until smooth and thickened, 2–3 minutes. Pour over the veal.

COVER THE BAKING DISH or Dutch oven and bake for 45 minutes. Uncover and continue to cook until the veal is tender when pierced with a fork, about 30 minutes longer.

JUST BEFORE THE MEAT IS DONE, melt the remaining butter in a large sauté pan over medium-high heat (there should be 3–4 tablespoons). Add the mushrooms and sauté, stirring and tossing constantly, until just tender, 3–4 minutes. Remove from the heat.

WHEN THE MEAT IS DONE, remove from the oven, uncover and gently stir in the cream, mixing well. Add the mushrooms, stirring to distribute evenly, and serve immediately. ❧

USE A COVERED ovenproof baking dish or Dutch oven to make this easy veal stew. I recommend you seek out a quality butcher who sells good white, milk-fed veal, as darker red veal is too strong flavored and meaty textured for the delicate seasonings and sauce.

CHICKEN BREASTS WITH RASPBERRY VINEGAR

SERVES 4

I came up with this quick recipe to show off the fresh, fruity flavor of French raspberry vinegar, which had become exceedingly popular among chefs in both Paris and New York. We began to import our raspberry vinegar from Paul Corcellet, a Parisian company established in 1760 to provide rare condiments to the king of France. The original Corcellet had been granted permission by the king to open his shop at the Palais Royal. Many years later the shop moved to its present location at Rue Norte Dame des Champs.

4 chicken breast halves, 8–9 oz each, skinned and boned
  (about 6 oz each when boned)
2 tablespoons unsalted butter
1 tablespoon vegetable oil
2 tablespoons minced shallot
⅓ cup (3 fl oz) chicken stock
¼ cup (2 fl oz) raspberry vinegar
⅓ cup (3 fl oz) heavy cream
salt and freshly ground pepper
chopped fresh parsley

TRIM ANY EXCESS FAT from the chicken breasts. Rinse and pat dry with paper towels. One at a time, place a chicken breast between 2 sheets of waxed paper or plastic wrap. Using a rolling pin, flatten to an even thickness of about ½ inch.

IN A SAUTÉ PAN or frying pan over medium-high heat, melt the butter with the oil. When hot, add the chicken breasts and sauté gently, turning once, until golden, opaque throughout and the juices run clear when pierced with a knife, about 3 minutes on each side. Transfer to a warmed plate and keep warm.

Raspberry Vinegar Mayonnaise

Have all the ingredients at room temperature. In a small bowl, whisk 1 egg yolk vigorously. While whisking, add 2 teaspoons raspberry vinegar and a little salt and white pepper. Measure ½ cup (4 fl oz) light, mild oil. Add 1 tablespoon to the yolk mixture and beat thoroughly. Start adding the remaining oil a little at a time, whisking to incorporate thoroughly after each addition. When all is incorporated and the sauce is thickened and smooth, season with salt and white pepper. Makes about ¾ cup.

POUR OFF EXCESS FAT from the pan and place over medium-low heat. Add the shallot and sauté, stirring, until translucent, 1–2 minutes. Add the stock and simmer, scraping up any bits stuck to the bottom of the pan, about 3 minutes. Add the vinegar, raise the heat to medium-high and bring to a boil. Cook until reduced by half, 3–4 minutes longer. Reduce the heat to medium-low, stir in the cream and cook until bubbling.

SEASON THE SAUCE to taste with salt and pepper and return the chicken breasts to the pan. Turn the chicken breasts in the sauce once or twice until well coated and heated through. Taste and adjust the seasonings. Serve immediately on warmed individual plates and sprinkle with parsley. ❧

Apple Pudding with Raspberry Vinegar

With its fresh, fruity taste, good raspberry vinegar also works well in sweet recipes such as this one: Peel, quarter, core and slice 4 cooking apples and place in a heavy saucepan. Add 1/2 cup water and 2 tablespoons sugar and cook slowly, stirring as needed to prevent scorching, until the apples are soft. Pass the apples through a food mill or sieve placed over a bowl and let cool. Add 1 1/2 cups (3 oz) fresh bread crumbs and 2 or 3 tablespoons raspberry vinegar and stir to mix. Transfer to a buttered 1-quart baking dish, sprinkle the top with Demerara sugar or light brown sugar and dot with knobs of butter. Bake in a 350°F oven until bubbly, 20–25 minutes. Serve with crème fraîche or whipped cream.

HERBES DE PROVENCE

Used to season the recipe on the right, herbes de Provence are a traditional blend of herbs from the south of France. You can buy them ready-mixed in little clay crocks from specialty-food stores, or make your own, using the most aromatic dried (not powdered) herbs you can find. For about ¼ cup herbes de Provence, stir together 2 tablespoons each of dried thyme, dried summer savory and dried basil, 1 teaspoon whole fennel seeds and ½ teaspoon dried lavender. You're most likely to find dried lavender in shops selling soaps and body lotions. Store in an airtight container. Try crumbling a pinch into olive oil that you use to sauté zucchini or potatoes, or sprinkle a little over meats or poultry destined for the oven or the outdoor grill.

VEGETABLES, HAM AND COUSCOUS

SERVES 4–6

On one of my early trips to Paris, my friend Mme Hermance Pomposi made a delicious dish of braised chicken served with couscous for a simple supper at her Paris flat on the Boulevard St. Germain. I was instantly taken with this tiny North African form of semolina pasta, which the French adopted during their colonial days. Traditional couscous takes a long time to cook, but the French also perfected the quick-cooking variety that has become popular here. It is now widely available and can be prepared in just a few minutes. If the tomatoes in this more traditional North African recipe don't give off enough liquid and the dish seems too dry, add a little more chicken stock.

3 tablespoons olive oil
2 yellow onions, thinly sliced
2 cloves garlic, chopped
1–1¼ lb cooked ham, cut into 1-inch dice
2 teaspoons herbes de Provence (see left)
3 celery stalks, sliced
2 lb tomatoes, peeled, seeded (see page 70) and chopped

1 green bell pepper, halved, seeded, deribbed and sliced crosswise
1 lb yellow summer squashes, sliced
salt and freshly ground pepper
1½ cups (12 fl oz) chicken stock
2 cups (10 oz) quick-cooking couscous
1 tablespoon fresh lemon juice
4 tablespoons (2 oz) unsalted butter

IN A SAUCEPAN over medium-low heat, warm the olive oil. Add the onions and garlic and sauté, stirring, until translucent, 7–10 minutes; do not allow to brown. Add the ham and herbes de Provence, stir well and cook for 1 minute. Raise the heat to medium, add the celery and tomatoes and cook, stirring occasionally, for 10 minutes. Add the green pepper and squash and cook, stirring, until all the vegetables are tender, about 5 minutes longer. Season to taste with salt and pepper.

MEANWHILE, pour the stock into a saucepan and bring to a boil over high heat. Put the couscous into a heatproof bowl. When the stock is boiling, pour it over the couscous and add the lemon juice and 2 tablespoons of the butter. Stir, cover and let stand until the stock is absorbed, 2–3 minutes. Uncover and fluff with a fork. In a sauté pan over low heat, melt the remaining 2 tablespoons butter. Add the couscous, stir and cover. Allow to steam over low heat for 2–3 minutes, stirring several times. Do not allow to brown.

TO SERVE, spoon the couscous onto warmed individual plates. Top with the vegetables-and-ham mixture. Serve at once. ҉

"My one unbreakable rule has always been to use only the freshest and finest ingredients available. Our quest for the freshest and best of the region has led us to Amador County for suckling pigs and wonderful, peppery watercress; to the Napa Valley for Zinfandel made especially for the restaurant; to Gilroy for garlic; to Sonoma County for locally made goat cheeses; to the ocean daily for oysters; to the backyards of our customers where we have our own gardens; and finally, if we must, to the local produce markets for that which we cannot grow or procure ourselves."

—Alice Waters, *The Chez Panisse Menu Cookbook* (1982)

"Good food has a magic appeal. You may grow old, even ugly, but if you are a good cook, people will always find the path to your door."

—James Beard

C.W. JOSEY'S TEXAS CHILI

SERVES 8–10

America's never-ending love affair with Tex-Mex food was going strong in the early 1980s, especially in Texas. I found that out when we started photographing the Williams-Sonoma catalog in Dallas. I discovered what real chili was all about from an authentic Texan, C.W. Josey, an award-winning chili maker and the father of a young woman who worked for Williams-Sonoma. He informed me that real Texans never add beans to their chili, and showed me what a great flavor you get when you season with pure ground red chili pepper and other spices and herbs instead of the ready-made blends sold in stores. Add chopped onion if you wish, sautéing it in the oil before adding the flour. If you like, serve the chili over boiled pinto beans or rice.

4 cups water
5 lb lean beef, cut into small cubes or coarsely ground
3 tablespoons sugar
2½ tablespoons salt
¼ cup (2 fl oz) olive oil
5 tablespoons (1½ oz) all-purpose flour
5 cloves garlic, chopped
6–8 tablespoons (1½ oz) pure ground dried red chili, or to taste
1 teaspoon freshly ground black pepper
2 teaspoons dried oregano
1 teaspoon ground cumin

IN A HEAVY SAUCEPAN over medium-high heat, combine the water, meat, sugar and salt. Bring to a boil, skim off any foam from the surface and immediately reduce the heat to medium-low so the meat is simmering gently. Do not allow to boil again.

IN A SMALL FRYING PAN over medium-low heat, warm the olive oil. Add the flour and cook, stirring constantly, for 2 minutes; do not allow to brown. Add the garlic, chili, black pepper, oregano and cumin and cook briefly, stirring, to release their fragrance. Add the flour mixture to the meat, stirring to blend, and simmer gently, uncovered, until the meat is tender, about 1½ hours.

TASTE AND ADJUST the seasonings, then serve. ☙

RANCHO EGGS

SERVES 4

Here's another recipe I picked up in Dallas for a popular Tex-Mex brunch dish. About halfway through the eggs' baking time, wrap corn or flour tortillas in aluminum foil and put them in the oven to heat up. Then transfer the tortillas to a napkin-lined basket and pass them when you serve the eggs.

2 tablespoons vegetable oil
1 or 2 cloves garlic, finely chopped
1 small yellow onion, finely chopped
2 lb tomatoes, peeled, seeded (see page 70) and chopped
1 mild or hot fresh green chili pepper, seeded and finely chopped
salt and freshly ground pepper
4–8 eggs
chopped fresh parsley

PREHEAT AN OVEN to 350°F.

IN A SAUCEPAN over medium-low heat, warm the vegetable oil. When hot, add the garlic and onion and sauté, stirring, until the onion is translucent, 7–10 minutes. Raise the heat to medium, add the tomatoes and chili pepper and cook, stirring occasionally, until some of the liquid has evaporated and the flavors are blended, about 5 minutes. Season to taste with salt and pepper.

SPOON THE TOMATO SAUCE into 4 ramekins, dividing it equally. Break 1 or 2 eggs into each dish. Bake until the eggs are set, 10–15 minutes. Remove from the oven, garnish with the parsley and serve at once. ҉

"America—unlike France, Italy, China and so on—does not have a national legacy of 'great' cooking that has been handed down from generation to generation. Many of its 'great' dishes are wholly regional—the gumbos and crawfish dishes of Louisiana, the Mexican-inspired foods of the Southwest, the chowders of New England. Most of American cooking is coarse, unpretentious and unsophisticated (grits, chili, clam chowder)."

—Craig Claiborne, *The New New York Times Cookbook* (1979)

STUFFED WHOLE ZUCCHINI

SERVES 4

In my unending quest for recipes to make use of zucchini from the garden, I found this dish in Italy. Cooks there use zucchini corers, which remove the seeds while leaving the vegetable whole. You can find them in specialty cookware shops. You can also use an apple corer, working it from both ends, or, with a little care, a slender paring knife. Take care not to break the skin, or the zucchini will fall apart during cooking.

8–10 zucchini, each about 6 inches long and 1½ inches
  in diameter
½ lb ground veal
1 egg
¼ cup (1 oz) freshly grated Parmesan cheese
½ cup (1 oz) fine fresh bread crumbs
3 tablespoons finely chopped cooked ham
freshly ground pepper
1 teaspoon chopped fresh oregano or ½ teaspoon dried oregano
2 tablespoons unsalted butter
1 tablespoon olive oil
1 yellow onion, chopped
1 tablespoon chopped fresh parsley
2 tablespoons tomato paste
1 cup water
1 bay leaf

CUT A SLICE from both ends of each zucchini, making them all the same length, approximately 5½ inches. Using a zucchini corer, a large apple corer or a slender-bladed paring knife, carefully hollow out the center of each zucchini, forming a hole ¾ inch in diameter, working from both ends if necessary and leaving the vegetable whole.

IN A BOWL, combine the veal, egg, Parmesan cheese, bread crumbs, ham, pepper to taste and oregano. Using a fork, mix well. Stuff the zucchini with this mixture, dividing it evenly.

IN A LARGE SAUTÉ PAN over medium-low heat, melt the butter with the oil. Add the onion and sauté, stirring, until translucent, 7–10 minutes. Raise the heat to medium, stir in the parsley, tomato paste and water and add the bay leaf. Simmer for 5 minutes. Add the zucchini in a single layer, cover and simmer, turning once, until the zucchini are tender when pierced, about 40 minutes.

Chuck Williams's 104th Recipe for Zucchini

First, toss a garlic clove into a heavy sauté pan with a little olive oil and let it cook for a minute or two. Add 2 large shallots, chopped, and sauté until just turning golden, 2–3 minutes. Then add 2 zucchini, diced fairly small, and sauté for 2–3 minutes. Add 3 slices Canadian bacon (or ham or prosciutto), chopped, and sauté briefly. Season to taste with salt and freshly ground pepper. Discard the garlic clove and toss this sauce with buttered, freshly cooked homemade pasta. Top with freshly grated Parmesan and eat immediately. Serves 2.

REMOVE THE BAY LEAF and discard. Transfer the zucchini to warmed individual plates or a serving platter and spoon the pan juices over the top. Serve immediately. ✧

BRAISED ENDIVE

SERVES 4

4 heads Belgian endive, bottoms trimmed
1 cup water
3 tablespoons unsalted butter, cut into small cubes
salt and freshly ground pepper
2 oz cooked ham, cut into strips 1 inch long and ½ inch wide
1–2 tablespoons fresh lemon juice
1 tablespoon chopped parsley

BRING A SAUCEPAN three-quarters full of water to a boil over high heat. Add the endives, reduce the heat to medium-low and simmer gently, uncovered, until half-cooked, 6–7 minutes.

DRAIN AND LAY the endives in a row in a sauté pan or deep frying pan. Add the 1 cup water to the pan and scatter half of the butter cubes over the endives. Sprinkle to taste with salt and pepper. Cover tightly and bring to a gentle simmer over medium-low heat. Simmer gently, basting occasionally, until very tender, 35–40 minutes. If the water begins to evaporate during cooking, add water to maintain original level.

PREHEAT A BROILER. Using a spatula, carefully transfer the endives to a flameproof baking dish, arranging them in a single row. Place the sauté pan or frying pan over high heat, bring the pan juices to a boil and reduce to a few spoonfuls, just a few minutes. Spoon the reduced juices over the endives. Scatter the ham strips and the remaining butter over the endives. Place the baking dish under the broiler 5–6 inches from the heat and broil, basting several times with the butter and juices in the dish, until golden, about 5 minutes.

DRIZZLE WITH THE LEMON JUICE to taste and garnish with the parsley. Serve at once directly from the dish. ✧

AMERICANS DISCOVERED Belgian endives on their travels to France in the 1950s and even earlier. But back home, the vegetable was expensive to buy—if you could find it at all. That changed during Williams-Sonoma's third decade, when some enterprising farmers began growing the pale yellow-green heads in the sandy soil of the New Jersey shore, where they thrived to yield a plentiful, more affordable crop. Now, with widespread distribution of perishable foods via air, you can buy Belgian endives practically everywhere. I recommend serving braised endive with steak au poivre with béarnaise sauce (recipe on page 65).

"My grandmother, who died at ninety-three, made pasta for us daily until the last few years of her life. At the end, when, instead of homemade pasta, an occasional dish of macaroni would appear on our table, she would be saddened and perplexed by our declining taste.

"There is no denying that, for a beginner, making pasta at home takes time, patience, and a considerable amount of physical effort. The rewards are such, however, that you should be persuaded to make the attempt. When you have mastered basic pasta dough you will have immediate access to some of the most miraculous creations in all gastronomy: *fettuccine,*

FETTUCCINE ALFREDO

SERVES 4

Fresh pasta, whether store-bought or made with an Atlas pasta machine, surged in popularity in the early 1980s. That led to the revival of a dish that owed as much to the Golden Age of Hollywood as it did to Italy. As I understand the story, silent-screen stars Mary Pickford and Douglas Fairbanks loved to visit Rome and dine where one of their favorite restauranteurs held forth. His name was Alfredo. One day he elaborated on the region's typical dish of fettuccine with butter and Parmesan by preparing this cream-enriched tableside creation especially for them. In response, they presented to him a gold fork and spoon in appreciation of such a memorable meal.

¾ cup (6 fl oz) heavy cream
2 tablespoons unsalted butter
2 tablespoons salt
10 oz fresh fettuccine (recipe on page 116)
½ cup (2 oz) freshly grated Italian Parmesan cheese, plus
  extra for the table
freshly ground pepper
freshly grated nutmeg

IN A LARGE SAUTE PAN over medium heat, combine the cream and butter. Bring to a simmer and continue to simmer for a few seconds, stirring until the cream and butter are blended. Remove from the heat and set aside; cover to keep warm.

BRING A LARGE SAUCEPAN three-fourths full of water to a rolling boil over high heat. Add the salt and fettuccine, stir gently, and quickly bring back to a boil. Boil until cooked, 15–30 seconds, then drain well. Add the pasta to the hot cream mixture along with the ½ cup Parmesan, pepper to taste and a few gratings of nutmeg. Place the sauté pan over high heat. Toss quickly until well blended and hot.

SERVE IMMEDIATELY on warmed individual plates. Pass additional Parmesan at the table. ♔

tortellini, cappelletti, cappellacci, tortelloni, cannelloni, lasagne, garganelli, and all their glorious variations. As you become skillful, you will discover, too, that the fresh egg pasta you are making at home is not only vastly better than what you can buy in any store, but that it is also superior to what you are likely to eat in any restaurant this side of the Alps."

—Marcella Hazan, *The Classic Italian Cook Book* (1976)

"[Fettuccini is] only flour, egg and water, even as the world is only land, sunlight and sea."

—Herb Caen, adored San Francisco columnist

FRESH PASTA

MAKES ABOUT 10 OZ FRESH NOODLES

1⅓ cups (7 oz) plus 2 tablespoons all-purpose flour, plus
  ½ cup (2½ oz) flour for rolling out pasta
2 eggs, lightly beaten

IN A FOOD PROCESSOR fitted with the metal blade, combine the 1⅓ cups plus 2 tablespoons flour and the eggs. Process, stopping to scrape down the sides of the bowl with a spatula as needed, until the mixture gathers together into a rough mass and can be pressed into a ball. Add more flour if the dough is too sticky, or a few drops of water if it is too dry. (Flours differ in how much moisture they absorb.) Gather the dough into a ball, then cut into 2 equal pieces. Form each half into a ball and cover with an inverted bowl until you are ready to roll it out.

SET THE ROLLERS OF A PASTA MACHINE on their widest opening. Dust the work surface next to the pasta machine with the ½ cup flour. Flatten a ball of dough with your palm, dust both sides with flour and feed it through the rollers. Fold in half and feed through the rollers again. Repeat 2 or 3 times, dipping the dough in flour, if needed, and folding in half each time, until the dough is smooth and silky. Don't be afraid of overhandling the dough—it benefits from lots of rolling. Cut the piece of dough into two equal lengths so it will be easier to manage.

NEXT, DECREASE THE WIDTH of the roller opening by a notch and run each length through the rollers twice, dusting with flour if necessary. Repeat, reducing the roller opening width one notch at a time and running the dough through, until the desired thickness is achieved. Remember that pasta expands when it is cooked, so you will want it to be quite thin. Cut each strip of rolled dough in half crosswise, resulting in 4 sheets each about 12 inches long by 4 inches wide. Rub flour onto both sides of each sheet to prevent sticking and shake off any excess. Repeat with the second ball of dough. You will have 8 sheets in all.

CHOOSE A CUTTER of the desired width and pass each sheet of dough through it. Heap the cut strands into loose "nests" on a wooden board until ready to use. ✿

WILD RICE WITH MUSHROOMS AND NUTS

SERVES 4–6

Not actually rice at all but the seeds of a different strain of grass, wild rice has an appealing nutlike flavor and texture. Although it has been around for a long time, it enjoyed a new popularity in the early 1980s. As consumer demand for wild rice grew, California farmers in the Sacramento delta began to cultivate it to supplement the limited supplies of the grain grown and/or gathered wild by Native Americans in Minnesota.

1½ cups (9 oz) wild rice
4 tablespoons (2 oz) unsalted butter
1 yellow onion, minced
3 cups (24 fl oz) chicken stock, heated
½ cup (2 oz) pecans
½ lb fresh mushrooms, wiped clean and sliced
2 teaspoons fresh lemon juice
¼ teaspoon freshly grated nutmeg
salt and freshly ground pepper

RINSE THE WILD RICE in three changes of water, then drain well; set aside. In a saucepan over medium-low heat, melt 2 tablespoons of the butter. When hot, add the onion and sauté, stirring, until translucent, 7–10 minutes; do not allow to brown. Add the wild rice and stir for a few seconds. Then add the stock, raise the heat to medium-high and bring to a boil. Reduce the heat to low, cover and simmer until the wild rice is tender and the liquid is absorbed, 55–60 minutes. Stir several times during cooking.

MEANWHILE, preheat an oven to 350°F. Spread the pecans on a baking sheet and toast until they begin to color and are fragrant, 5–10 minutes. Let cool and chop. Set aside.

JUST BEFORE THE WILD RICE IS COOKED, melt the remaining 2 tablespoons butter in a sauté pan over medium-high heat. When hot, add the mushrooms and sauté, stirring constantly, until lightly browned and tender, about 3 minutes.

ADD THE MUSHROOMS, lemon juice, nutmeg and pecans to the cooked rice and stir gently to mix. Season to taste with salt and pepper. Transfer to a warmed serving bowl and serve immediately. ♛

Spezzatino di Manzo Rapido (Quick Round Steak with Cream)

❧

I picked up this very fast recipe on one of my buying trips to Italy, and found it a great topping for fresh homemade pasta.

Peel and chop 2 onions and cook lightly in a sauté pan with 2 tablespoons unsalted butter. Trim any excess fat from about 1½ lb round steak and cut into 1-inch pieces. Add to the onion and stir until the meat is lightly seared. Add 2 tomatoes, peeled, seeded (see page 70) and chopped; 1 cup water; salt and freshly ground pepper to taste and a little thyme or other herb. Cover and simmer until tender, about 1 hour. Add about ¾ cup (6 fl oz) heavy cream and heat through. Serve at once over fresh pasta. Serves 6.

"Few Romans care much either about the gastronomic split between Italy's north and south; they know their own cuisine encompasses both tastes. One example of this eclecticism is *gnocchi,* a dish that is unclassifiable as either northern or southern. *Gnocchi* exists in many forms in many places, but it is especially esteemed in Rome, where it is made with flour and without the potatoes used elsewhere. The dish has a doughy, uninspired look that helps explain the dialect meaning of *gnocco* (the singular of *gnocchi*): 'dullard,' or 'puddinghead.' But its appearance belies its taste."

—Waverley Root, *The Cooking of Italy* (1968)

SEMOLINA GNOCCHI

SERVES 6 AS A FIRST COURSE, OR 4 AS A LIGHT MAIN COURSE

Most Americans think of the Italian dumplings known as gnocchi as being made strictly from a mixture of potatoes and flour, to which spinach is sometimes added. As our knowledge of Italian regional cooking grew in the late 1970s and early 1980s, we learned a few more subtleties behind the dish. In the Veneto in northwestern Italy, for example, gnocchi may be based on polenta (see page 157). In Rome, the source of this recipe, they are made from semolina, the coarse-grained hard-wheat flour also used for pasta.

4 cups (32 fl oz) milk
¼ teaspoon salt
freshly grated nutmeg
freshly ground pepper
1½ cups (9 oz) semolina flour
1 cup (4 oz) freshly grated Parmesan cheese, preferably Italian
2 eggs, beaten
4 tablespoons (2 oz) unsalted butter, melted

BUTTER A BAKING SHEET with sides and set aside.

POUR THE MILK into a deep saucepan over medium heat and heat until small bubbles appear around the edges of the pan. Add the salt and the nutmeg and pepper to taste. Using a wooden spoon and stirring constantly, slowly pour in the semolina. Reduce the heat to low and continue to cook, stirring and scraping the sides and bottom of the pan each time, until smooth and thick, 10–12 minutes. It should be thick enough for the spoon to stand upright in the mixture.

REMOVE FROM THE HEAT and stir in ¾ cup of the Parmesan cheese, then gradually add the beaten eggs, stirring vigorously to prevent them from coagulating. Taste and adjust the seasonings. Immediately pour the mixture onto the prepared pan. Using a wet rubber spatula or spoon, spread out the mixture evenly. It should be about ½ inch thick. Set aside to cool, then cover and refrigerate for several hours until very cold and firm.

PREHEAT AN OVEN to 450°F. Butter a large shallow, oval or round baking dish.

USING A ROUND COOKIE CUTTER 1¼ inches in diameter, cut out rounds of the firm semolina. Arrange the rounds in overlapping concentric circles in the prepared dish. (If you have a square or rectangular dish, arrange the rounds in straight rows.) Drizzle the melted butter evenly over the top, then sprinkle with the remaining ¼ cup Parmesan cheese.

BAKE UNTIL CRISP, browned and bubbly, 15–20 minutes. Serve immediately on warmed individual plates. ♨

Freshly grated nutmeg has so much more flavor than the already ground stuff. Buy whole nutmegs and grate them as needed with the fine rasps of a nutmeg grater, which includes a little compartment for holding the spice when not in use.

"I am not alone in my feeling that home is not only the most natural but the most evocative place to entertain . . . In the decade I have been a professional caterer, there has been a culinary revolution. It has taught us to appreciate the aesthetics of food —the fresh, the simple, the home-made—and shown us the possibilities of many different tastes and styles. It has made food an adventure to be shared. It has also fostered a new style of entertaining that is informal, relaxed, and expressive, based not on intimidating prescriptions and pretensions, but on personality and personal effect."

—Martha Stewart, *Entertaining* (1982)

FOCACCIA CON OLIO E SALE

MAKES ONE 10-BY-15-INCH SHEET; SERVES 6–8

The Italian flat bread called focaccia, a rustic cousin to the pizza, found a huge following here in the mid-1980s, fueled by Italian boutique bakeries across the country. It is good served hot at breakfast with fried or scrambled eggs or at lunch alongside a salad or soup. Or use the focaccia for making wonderful sandwiches, either open-faced or closed. Pair it with tissue-thin slices of prosciutto and your favorite Italian cheese.

3¼ cups (16½ oz) unbleached bread flour
2 teaspoons quick-rise yeast
1 teaspoon salt
3 tablespoons extra-virgin olive oil, plus extra for brushing
1¼ cups warm water (110°F), or as needed
4 fresh rosemary sprigs
coarse sea salt, optional

IN A LARGE BOWL, combine the flour, yeast and salt. Using a wooden spoon, stir to mix well. Add the 3 tablespoons olive oil. Then, while stirring, gradually add the 1¼ cups warm water until all of the flour has been absorbed and a dough forms. You may not need all of the water or you may need a bit more.

USING YOUR HANDS, gather the dough into a ball and transfer to a well-floured work surface. Knead until soft and elastic and no longer sticky, about 10 minutes. Work more flour into the dough if needed to reduce stickiness; be sure to keep the work surface well floured. Place the dough in a warmed, lightly oiled bowl, turning several times to coat it with oil. Cover with plastic wrap and let rise in a warm place until doubled in bulk, 45–75 minutes.

POSITION A RACK in the lower third of an oven and preheat to 400°F. Brush a 10-by-15-inch baking pan with ½-inch sides with olive oil and set aside.

PUNCH DOWN THE DOUGH and transfer to the floured surface. Knead a few times, then let rest for 5–6 minutes. With the palms of your hands, form into a rectangle about 4 by 8 inches. Roll out the dough to fit the prepared pan. Transfer the dough to the pan. Stretch and pat the dough to cover the pan bottom completely with an even thickness. Cover with plastic wrap; let rise until about 1 inch high, 20–30 minutes.

USING YOUR FINGERTIPS, make "dimple" indentations in the dough, spacing them 2 inches apart. Remove the leaves from the rosemary sprigs and either leave them whole or chop them. Brush the surface with olive oil and sprinkle lightly with the rosemary and coarse sea salt, if desired.

BAKE UNTIL GOLDEN BROWN, 30–40 minutes. Transfer to a rack and let cool in the pan for a few minutes.

CUT INTO SQUARES and serve warm or at room temperature. To reheat, place in a preheated 300°F oven for 6–8 minutes. ҉

"No one knows who invented the first focaccia, but the contribution, like the discovery of fire or creation of the wheel, has enriched the experience of the civilization that followed."

—Carol Field,
Focaccia (1994)

121

CHOCOLATE BREAD

MAKES 1 LOAF

One of the bakers at Il Fornaio gave me this recipe for a delicious break-fast bread. I had to adapt it, however, because the original called for 16 kilos (over 35 pounds) of flour. I find that the tiny chocolate morsels work best here. You might want to try baking the bread in a clay cloche (see page 45), which will make it rise more and develop a better crust. If using a clay cloche, start with the oven temperature at 450°F. Bake the bread for 15 minutes, then reduce the oven temperature to 375°F and continue to bake for 25 minutes longer.

1 package (2½ teaspoons) active dry yeast
2 tablespoons sugar
1¼ cups lukewarm water (110°F)
4 cups (1¼ lb) all-purpose flour
⅓ cup (1 oz) Dutch-process unsweetened cocoa
2 teaspoons salt
1 egg, lightly beaten
2 tablespoons unsalted butter, at room temperature
1 cup (6 oz) small dark chocolate morsels

IN A SMALL BOWL, dissolve the yeast and 1 teaspoon of the sugar in ¼ cup of the lukewarm water and let stand until foamy, about 3 minutes.

IN THE BOWL of a heavy-duty stand mixer, combine the flour, cocoa and salt. Using a wooden spoon, stir in the yeast mixture, egg, butter, the remaining 5 teaspoons sugar and the remaining 1 cup lukewarm water. Fit the mixer with a dough hook and knead on medium speed until the dough is smooth and supple, about 10 minutes. Turn out the dough onto a lightly floured work surface and knead by hand for 1 minute, adding a little more flour if the dough is sticky. The dough must be quite firm and not sticky, as it must hold its shape when formed into a loaf. Knead in the chocolate morsels.

ALTERNATIVELY, combine the flour, cocoa and salt in a large bowl and stir with a wooden spoon to mix. Then stir in the yeast mixture, egg, butter, the remaining 5 teaspoons sugar and the remaining 1 cup lukewarm water to form a dough that holds its shape. Turn out the dough onto a floured work surface and knead by hand until smooth and supple yet firm, about 10 minutes, adding a little flour if the dough is sticky. Knead in the chocolate morsels.

WARM A BOWL with hot water, dry with a kitchen towel and coat the inside with butter. Shape the dough into a ball, place in the prepared bowl, cover with buttered plastic wrap and let rise in a warm place until doubled in bulk, 1–1½ hours.

BUTTER A BAKING PAN. Turn out the dough onto the floured work surface, punch down and knead for 1 minute. Let rest for 5 minutes. Form into an 8-by-4-inch oval and place on the prepared baking pan. Cover loosely with buttered plastic wrap and let rise in a warm place until doubled in bulk, about 1 hour.

MEANWHILE, preheat an oven to 375°F.

REMOVE THE PLASTIC WRAP and place the pan in the oven. Bake until the loaf is browned and sounds hollow when tapped on the underside, 40–45 minutes. Transfer to a wire rack to cool. ❦

"To knead bread is an emotional experience; to eat fresh bread is a sensual delight."

—James Beard

WALNUT BREAD

MAKES 1 LOAF

This is another recipe originally supplied to me by the bakers at Il Fornaio. The bread is wonderful thinly sliced, toasted and served with a creamy Italian cheese such as Gorgonzola dolcelatte.

2½ cups (10 oz) walnuts
1 package (2½ teaspoons) active dry yeast
1½ cups lukewarm water (110°F)
3 cups (15 oz) unbleached bread flour
2 cups (10 oz) whole-wheat bread flour
1 tablespoon salt
2 tablespoons olive oil
2 tablespoons dark molasses
yellow cornmeal

PREHEAT AN OVEN to 350°F. Spread the walnuts on a baking sheet and toast until they begin to color and are fragrant, 5–10 minutes. Remove from the oven, let cool and chop coarsely.

IN A SMALL BOWL, dissolve the yeast in ¼ cup of the lukewarm water and let stand until foamy, about 3 minutes. In a large bowl, using a wooden spoon, mix together the flours, salt and toasted walnuts. Stir in the yeast mixture, the remaining 1¼ cups lukewarm water, the olive oil and the molasses. Mix thoroughly, adding more water or flour as necessary to produce a smooth dough. Turn out the dough onto a floured work surface and knead by hand until smooth, satiny and not sticky, about 15 minutes.

WARM A BOWL with hot water and dry with a kitchen towel. Shape the dough into a ball, place in the bowl, cover with plastic wrap and let rise in a warm place until doubled in bulk, 45–75 minutes.

SPRINKLE A BAKING SHEET with cornmeal. Turn out the dough onto the floured work surface, punch down and knead for 1 minute. Form into an oval loaf and place on the prepared baking sheet. Cover with a damp cloth and let rise again until doubled in bulk, 30–40 minutes. Meanwhile, preheat an oven to 425°F.

REMOVE THE CLOTH and place the pan in the oven. Bake for 15 minutes. Reduce the oven temperature to 375°F and continue to bake until the loaf is browned and sounds hollow when tapped on the underside, 30–40 minutes longer. Transfer to a wire rack to cool. ✾

Parsley Butter

Drop by drop, beat 2 tablespoons lemon juice into ½ cup (4 oz) softened unsalted butter. Then beat in 3 tablespoons minced parsley. Season with a little salt. Form into a roll and refrigerate. Spread on hot crusty bread or use as a topping for freshly cooked vegetables.

ALMOND COOKIES

MAKES ABOUT 40 SMALL COOKIES

Quick and easy to make, these are among my favorite little cookies. Offer them with coffee or tea, or serve them along with ice cream, sorbet or fresh fruit.

½ cup (2¾ oz) almonds
½ cup (4 oz) unsalted butter
½ cup (4 oz) sugar
1 teaspoon vanilla extract
finely grated zest of ½ lemon
1 egg white
⅔ cup whole-wheat flour
¼ teaspoon ground ginger

PREHEAT AN OVEN to 325°F. Spread the almonds on a baking sheet and toast until they begin to color and are fragrant, 5–10 minutes. Remove from the oven and let cool. Using a nut mill, grind to a powder. (If you do not have a nut mill, use a blender or food processor fitted with the metal blade, adding a few tablespoons of the flour and being careful not to overprocess or the oils will be released and the nuts will turn to a paste.) Raise the oven temperature to 375°F. Position a rack in the upper part of the oven.

IN A BOWL, combine the butter and sugar. Using an electric mixer set on medium speed, beat until light and creamy, about 5 minutes. Add the vanilla and lemon zest and beat briefly to combine. Then beat in the egg white. In another bowl, stir together the ground nuts, flour and ginger. Add to the butter-sugar mixture and beat until smooth.

USING A TEASPOON, drop the batter by spoonfuls onto an ungreased baking sheet, spacing them about 2 inches apart. Place on the upper rack in the oven and bake until browned around the edges, about 10 minutes. Transfer to a wire rack to cool. Store in an airtight container for up to 2 weeks. ♛

NUT MILLS

If you make pastries regularly, an old-fashioned nut mill is an invaluable piece of equipment. A clamp attaches the enameled-steel device to the edge of a countertop. Shelled nuts go into its hopper, where they are pressed against a tinned-steel grating drum that is rotated with a hand crank. Out comes a soft, perfectly even-textured cloud of nut flour, without any loss of the nuts' oils. You can't make a Viennese torte without one!

"In moments of considerable strain I tend to take to bread-and-butter pudding. There is something about the blandness of soggy bread, the crispness of the golden outer crust and the unadulterated pleasure of a lightly set custard that makes the world seem a better place to live."

—Clement Freud,
Freud on Food (1978)

FRENCH BREAD AND BUTTER CUSTARD

SERVES 6–8

The French have always been ingenious about using up leftover bread to make something delicious. Think of French toast, for example, and you'll be halfway to imagining what this dessert is like. Here, more eggs are used along with egg yolks to form a rich custard. The bread soaks up a little of the custard and floats on the top, turning brown and crusty. One of the best versions I ever tasted was the one Alice B. Toklas put in her famous cookbook, which calls for the rich butter-and-egg bread known as brioche.

about 6 slices day-old French bread, each ½ inch thick
unsalted butter, at room temperature
2 cups (16 fl oz) heavy cream
2 cups (16 fl oz) milk
2 lemon zest strips, each about 2 inches long and ¼ inch wide
⅓ vanilla bean, slit halfway through lengthwise to expose the seeds
3 whole eggs, plus 4 egg yolks
½ cup (4 oz) granulated sugar
2 tablespoons slivered blanched almonds
confectioners' sugar

PREHEAT AN OVEN to 325°F.

BRING A TEAKETTLE full of water to a boil. Butter a 2-quart oval or rectangular baking dish about 2 inches deep. Place the prepared dish in a baking pan about 3 inches deep that will accommodate it comfortably.

TRIM THE BREAD SLICES (do not remove the crusts) so that they will fit closely together to cover the custard completely once it is poured into the baking dish. The slices must not overlap, however. Butter the slices on one side only; set aside.

IN A LARGE SAUCEPAN over medium heat, combine the cream, milk, lemon zest and vanilla bean. Heat until small bubbles appear around the edges of the pan. Remove from the heat and set aside to cool for 5–6 minutes.

IN A LARGE BOWL, combine the whole eggs, egg yolks and granulated sugar. Using a whisk, beat until blended and a light lemon color, about 5 minutes. Remove the lemon zest and the vanilla bean from the hot cream-milk mixture and discard. Gradually add the hot cream-milk mixture to the beaten egg mixture while stirring constantly until blended. Then pour the mixture into the prepared baking dish. Carefully float the prepared bread slices on top of the custard, buttered side up. Scatter the slivered almonds over the bread slices.

POUR BOILING WATER into the pan to reach halfway up the sides of the dish. Bake until the bread slices are golden and crusty on top and a knife blade inserted into the center of the custard comes out clean, 40–45 minutes. Transfer to a wire rack to cool. The custard is best served warm or at room temperature. Using a sifter or sieve, dust the top with confectioners' sugar just before serving. ✧

Papaya Cream

French cooks have always had a fascination for tropical fruits, and this dessert is a good example of how easily they can transform them into something pretty and delicious.

Purée 3 cups (18 oz) peeled, seeded and chopped papaya. In a heatproof bowl, soften 2 packages (1 tablespoon each) unflavored gelatin in 1/3 cup cold water. Place over (but not touching) hot water in a saucepan until the gelatin dissolves. Add 1/3 cup of the papaya and 1 cup (8 oz) sugar to the gelatin; stir until smooth. Add the balance of the papaya, the juice of 2 limes, and the zest of 1 lime, cut into narrow strips and blanched (immersed in boiling water for 3 minutes and drained). Fold 2 cups (16 fl oz) heavy cream, whipped, into the papaya mixture. Pour into a soufflé dish wrapped with a paper collar (see page 44) and chill until set. Before serving, remove the collar and decorate the top or sides with kiwifruit slices.

CHUCK'S ORANGES IN SYRUP

SERVES 6

Whenever I traveled through Italy in the 1970s, I always admired the bowls of whole peeled oranges in an orange zest–flavored syrup that restaurants often displayed on their dessert tables. This is the same idea, only I've made the oranges easier to eat by cutting them into slices before putting them in the syrup. The almond cookies on page 125 would make a good accompaniment, as would a cup of espresso.

6 oranges
1½ cups (12 oz) sugar
¾ cup water
2 teaspoons Grand Marnier or other orange-flavored liqueur

USING A VEGETABLE PEELER or a paring knife, carefully cut off the zest (orange part only) in strips from 2 of the oranges. Cut the strips into toothpick-wide pieces about 1 inch long. Bring a small saucepan three-fourths full of water to a boil, add the zest strips and boil for 5 minutes. Drain and set aside.

CUT A THICK SLICE off the top and bottom of each orange, exposing the fruit beneath the peel. Working with 1 orange at a time, place upright on a work surface and, holding the orange firmly, thickly slice off the peel in wide strips, cutting off the pith and membrane with it to reveal the fruit sections. Cut the orange crosswise into slices 1 inch thick and place in a large, heatproof glass bowl. Repeat with remaining oranges.

IN A HEAVY SAUCEPAN over medium heat, combine the sugar and water. Bring slowly to a boil, stirring to dissolve the sugar. Boil until slightly thickened, 10–15 minutes. Add the reserved zest and cook for 1–2 minutes longer. Stir in the Grand Marnier or other liqueur and pour over the orange slices. Let stand for several hours in a cool place. Cover and refrigerate to chill slightly before serving. ꕥ

Livorno Custard

This typical Italian custard would also make a nice dessert buffet companion to the oranges at right.

Put 4 cups (32 fl oz) half-and-half and 2 strips orange zest in a saucepan. Heat until small bubbles appear around the edges of the pan, remove from the heat and let cool. Discard the zest. Beat 6 egg yolks and 3 whole eggs with ½ cup (4 oz) sugar until light. Gradually add the half-and-half, whisking until well blended. Stir in 2 tablespoons Galliano liqueur. Pour into custard cups and place them in a baking pan. Add boiling water to reach halfway up the sides of the cups, cover with foil and bake in a 300°F oven until set, about 1 hour. Serves 6.

SIMPLE CHOCOLATE TRUFFLES

MAKES ABOUT 50 TRUFFLES

Alice Medrich, with her book and chocolate shop in Berkeley, California, both named Cocolat, began to excite everyone about chocolate truffles in the early 1980s. Hers were small and intense, true to the French ideal. I like to use a good French or Belgian chocolate such as Valrhona or Callebaut for these.

½ cup (4 oz) unsalted butter, cut into small cubes
8 oz bittersweet or semisweet chocolate, chopped
¼ cup (2 fl oz) heavy cream
½ cup (1½ oz) Dutch-process unsweetened cocoa

IN A SMALL SAUCEPAN over very low heat, melt the butter, watching carefully so it does not burn. Remove from the heat and let stand for a minute to settle, then carefully skim the foam from the top and discard. Pour the remaining yellow liquid into a cup, leaving the milky solids behind in the pan. The clear yellow liquid is clarified butter; set aside to cool. Discard the milky solids.

PLACE THE CHOCOLATE in a heatproof bowl or the top pan of a double boiler. Set over (but not touching) hot or barely simmering water in a saucepan or the bottom pan of the double boiler. Stir gently until the chocolate is melted and smooth. Remove from over the water. Add the clarified butter to the chocolate and stir until blended. Stir the cream into the chocolate. Cover and place in the refrigerator to thicken for 10–15 minutes.

SPREAD THE COCOA in a dish. Using a teaspoon, scoop up a rounded spoonful of the thickened chocolate and, with the aid of a second teaspoon, shape into a ¾-inch piece. Drop the piece into the cocoa and turn to coat. Transfer to a plate or tray. Repeat until all the chocolate has been used, then refrigerate to harden for 30–40 minutes. When the pieces are firm enough to handle, shape them with your fingers into roundish balls and roll in the cocoa again until completely covered. Place in a storage container. Pour any remaining cocoa over the truffles and shake the container to distribute the cocoa evenly. Cover and return to the refrigerator for up to 1 week. Remove from the refrigerator about 10 minutes before serving. ♛

Truffle Elaborations

You can produce all kinds of flavored truffles without any more effort than you put into making plain chocolate ones. Here are a few suggestions:

Grand Marnier Truffles
Place the cream in a small saucepan with 3 strips of orange zest, each 3 inches long and ¼ inch wide. Warm over medium heat until small bubbles appear around the edges of the pan, then remove from the heat and let cool completely. Discard the orange zest and add the cream to the warm chocolate-butter mixture. Then stir in 2 tablespoons Grand Marnier or other orange-flavored liqueur.

Rum or Cognac Truffles
Stir 2 tablespoons dark rum or Cognac into the warm chocolate-cream mixture.

Espresso Truffles
Stir 1 teaspoon instant espresso powder into the warm chocolate-cream mixture.

White Chocolate Mint Truffles
Substitute a good-quality white chocolate for the bittersweet or semisweet chocolate. Stir 2 tablespoons white crème de menthe liqueur into the warm chocolate-cream mixture.

GINO COFACCI'S CHOCOLATE RUM CHEESECAKE

MAKES ONE 9-INCH CAKE; SERVES 10–12

A friend and student of James Beard, Gino Cofacci became an excellent pastry cook. Among his greatest creations is this cheesecake. He made it for several top restaurants in New York City and won quite a following. Although his name is Italian, Gino's recipe is thoroughly American. Yet, its use of chocolate and rum shows how innovative we were becoming even with our old standards. The outside of the pan is covered with aluminum foil to reflect heat away from the cheesecake, thus slowing down the cooking and resulting in a more evenly baked cake. When you take the cheesecake out of the oven, its center may look too soft, but it will firm up as it cools.

1¼ cups (3¾ oz) graham cracker crumbs
2 tablespoons plus ¾ cup (6 oz) sugar
¼ cup (2 oz) unsalted butter, melted
6 oz semisweet chocolate, chopped
¼ cup (2 fl oz) dark rum
1 lb cream cheese, at room temperature
½ cup (4 fl oz) sour cream

1 tablespoon vanilla extract

5 eggs

PREHEAT AN OVEN to 325°F. Generously butter the inside of a 9-inch springform pan and cover the outside (bottom and sides) with a sheet of heavy-duty aluminum foil, shiny side out.

IN A SMALL BOWL, stir together the graham cracker crumbs and the 2 tablespoons sugar. Gradually add the melted butter, stirring constantly until the crumbs are evenly coated. Place in the prepared pan and press evenly over the bottom and about two-thirds up the sides of the pan. Refrigerate until ready to fill.

PLACE THE CHOCOLATE and rum in a heatproof bowl or in the top pan of a double boiler. Set the bowl or pan over (but not touching) barely simmering water in a saucepan or the bottom pan of the double boiler. Stir gently until the chocolate is melted and smooth. Remove from over the water and set aside to let cool completely.

PLACE THE CREAM CHEESE in a heatproof bowl. Using an electric mixer set on medium speed, beat until light and fluffy and no lumps remain, about 10 minutes. Gradually beat in the ¾ cup sugar, the sour cream and vanilla. Add the eggs one at a time, beating thoroughly after each addition. Set the bowl over (but not touching) hot water in a saucepan off the heat and stir gently with a wooden spoon to dispel any bubbles, continuing to stir until the mixture is completely smooth, 10–15 minutes. Pour about 1¼ cups of this batter into a separate bowl and set aside. Carefully stir the chocolate mixture into the remaining batter until blended.

REMOVE THE PREPARED SPRINGFORM PAN from the refrigerator and pour the chocolate batter into it. Carefully and slowly pour the plain batter over the top. Using a thin wooden skewer, make swirls down into the chocolate batter. Bake until puffed and no longer shiny, about 50 minutes. Transfer to a wire rack and let cool completely. Remove the foil, then remove the pan sides. Cover and refrigerate overnight before serving. ✼

Frozen Coffee Mousse

Easily a decade or more before the quality coffee craze swept the nation, this simple frozen dessert was created for coffee-lovers.

In a saucepan, combine 1 cup extra-strong brewed coffee, ³/₄ cup (6 oz) sugar, 1 teaspoon gelatin and a small pinch of salt. Stir over low heat until the sugar and gelatin dissolve. Pour into a bowl, cover and chill until syrupy and somewhat thickened. Fold in 2 cups (16 fl oz) heavy cream, whipped, and spoon into a 1-quart charlotte mold. Freeze until firm, unmold and decorate with chocolate curls.

1986–1996

BACK TO THE BASICS

It's harder to sum up the most recent decade, simply because you need more distance to arrive at a clear perspective on any era. Still, looking back on these years, I can recognize some significant trends: an increase of interest in simpler and healthier food and a return to the basics of good home cooking.

During the late 1980s and early 1990s, cooks everywhere were striving to prepare recipes that were less complicated. All over the country I saw old-fashioned diners cooking up roast turkey, garlic mashed potatoes and apple crisp; simple French bistros offering lentils and sausages and *crème brûlée*; and authentic Italian trattorias serving pizza, risotto and linguine with pesto. It was also the decade of the muffin and of boutique bakeries, with their loaves of European-style bread of every description.

It is significant to note that publishers responded with updated versions of the classics we'd seen our moms and grandmothers use, including a completely revised and modernized edition of *The New Settlement Cookbook* (1991) and Marion Cunningham's 1990 revision of *The Fannie Farmer Cookbook.* Some of the country's best chefs and authors brought out new books with a comfortingly retro philosophy, in particular Joyce Goldstein's *Back to Square One* (1992). You can see that same demand for down-to-earth simplicity in the Williams-Sonoma Kitchen Library, which we launched in 1992 and, as I write this now, has already sold over six million copies.

Journalists were quick to tell us that this trend was a reaction to the end of the boom years of the 1980s and the start of economic belt-tightening; I'm sure there is some truth to that. But I think the reason is even more basic: all those serious cooks of the previous decade were just settling down and letting their interest in cooking find its own natural level.

Dessert making also experienced a renaissance in these years. We went mad for chocolate like never before, a craze reflected in such books as Alice Medrich's *Cocolat* (1990), *Glorious Chocolate* (1989) by Mary Goodbody and the staff of *Chocolatier* magazine, and Marcel Desaulnier's vividly titled *Death By Chocolate* (1992). A number of important baking books came out, too, with one of the best *The Cake Bible* (1988) by Rose Levy Berenbaum. Without a doubt, though, the top baking book of the decade was Flo Braker's *The Simple Art of Perfect Baking,* which appeared in a revised edition in 1992.

One of the reasons baking took off owes to the desire of hosts to make a good impression on their guests. Entertaining as an expression of lifestyle explains the continued popularity of authors like Martha Stewart and Lee Bailey, who seem to come out with new books every year that show you how creative home cooking and casual, stylish living go together. It also explains the rise in lavishly produced, full-color volumes like the Beautiful Cookbook series, which reflect their owners' strong interest in good food and travel.

Every year we have become more serious about healthy eating as well. You can't pick up a newspaper today without finding mention

of some study that reports the
effects of fats, salt or fiber on our
diets. In 1991, the United States
Departments of Agriculture and of
Health and Human Services jointly
released a Food Guide Pyramid that
outlined a healthful diet high in complex carbohydrates, vegetables and
fruits and low in fats and sugars.

Chefs and authors alike got the message. Upscale restaurants around
the country now make sure their menus include healthful selections.
Juice bars have replaced lunch counters. More cookbooks than ever
before emphasize health-conscious principles. And who would have
thought that the hottest trend in supermarket chains would be the
stocking of healthy foods, from salad bars to organic produce and
hormone-free meats.

The fact that home cooks and professionals alike now routinely
prepare reduced-fat versions of classic recipes suggests another trend:
a confidence among American cooks that lets them take liberties
like never before. You can see this going on, for example, in the
many restaurants today that bill their food as Pacific Rim cuisine and
combine, say, Japanese and Chinese specialties with those of California, the Pacific Northwest or Mexico.

We have come a long way as cooks during the last 40 years, traveling far beyond those early trips to France and Italy. The pots and
tools we once bought now have become family heirlooms. We've
planted kitchen gardens and assembled libraries of cookbooks whose authors now feel like cherished friends.
Today, in short, there are more opportunities than
ever for all of us to enjoy the pleasures of cooking.

Entertaining has be-
come an expression
of lifestyle.

Cheese and Onion Casserole

Cheese and onions are wonderful together. Here's another, even easier recipe for the pairing, which has run in several different versions in the Williams-Sonoma catalog over the years. Slice 2 large yellow onions into a shallow pan. Add 2 tablespoons unsalted butter and enough water to keep the onions from burning. Cook over low heat, stirring occasionally, until the onions are translucent, 6–8 minutes. Butter a large baking dish and arrange a layer of the onions in the bottom. Shred 1/4 lb Gruyère cheese and sprinkle some of it over the onions. Repeat the layers until onions and cheese are used up, finishing with a layer of the cheese. Bake in a preheated 325°F oven until the cheese and onions have melded and the top is slightly browned, about 30 minutes. Serve at once with French bread.

ROQUEFORT ONION CUSTARDS

SERVES 4

Elizabeth David made these custards for me around 1986. It is just the sort of marvelous dish she would cook and serve for lunch while you were sitting around and talking in her London kitchen. I think this recipe shows how, after all our travels and culinary discoveries of the previous decades, Americans have begun to appreciate simple foods. It is also another example of Elizabeth's love of nutmeg (see page 83).

2 or 3 green onions, including some of the tender green tops, coarsely chopped
1/2 cup (4 fl oz) milk
5 oz Roquefort cheese
1/3 cup (3 fl oz) heavy cream
2 eggs
freshly ground pepper
freshly grated nutmeg
boiling water, as needed

PREHEAT AN OVEN to 350°F. Have ready four 1/2-cup ramekins.

IN A SMALL SAUCEPAN over medium heat, combine the green onions and milk and heat until small bubbles appear around the edges of the pan. Remove from the heat and set aside to cool.

CRUMBLE THE CHEESE into a bowl and then mash it with a fork. Add the cream and stir gently. In a separate bowl, using a fork, beat the eggs until blended. Add the cooled milk and onions and mix well. Add the egg mixture to the cheese mixture, stirring to combine, then add pepper and nutmeg to taste. Do not overmix.

FILL THE RAMEKINS with the mixture, dividing it evenly, and place them in a baking pan. Add boiling water to the baking pan to reach two-thirds up the sides of the cups. Bake until the custards set and the tops are puffy and lightly browned, 25–30 minutes. Remove from the oven and serve warm. ✸

ROASTED GARLIC

SERVES 4

One of the biggest culinary trends of the past decade came about when small earthenware garlic roasters appeared around 1993. Suddenly, roasting whole heads of garlic was in. You can serve the garlic as an appetizer, accompanied with toasted country bread and a robust red wine.

4 whole heads garlic
3–4 tablespoons olive oil
2 teaspoons minced fresh oregano
salt

PREHEAT AN OVEN to 350°F. Remove any loose papery skin from the garlic heads and trim the root ends a little so the heads will stand upright. Cut off a little of the top to reveal the flesh. Arrange the garlic heads, root ends down, in a small baking dish. Drizzle the oil evenly over the top of each head and sprinkle with the oregano and salt to taste. Bake, uncovered, until the flesh is soft when pierced with a toothpick, 1–1½ hours. Remove from the oven and let cool for a few minutes.

TO SERVE, loosen the cloves, pulling them apart slightly but leaving the heads intact. Place on individual plates and spoon any hot oil remaining in the baking dish over the tops. Serve immediately. ✸

CREAM OF MUSHROOM SOUP WITH BRIE

SERVES 4

Here's a classic French recipe for mushroom soup, made different and interesting by adding slices of Brie cheese that are allowed to melt into each serving. That variation was given to me by Cheryl Schultz, who once managed our Dallas store and gave cooking classes there.

1 lb small, fresh mushrooms, preferably brown
¼ cup (2 oz) unsalted butter
2 tablespoons chopped shallot
1 small white sweet onion, chopped
1 white potato, peeled and cut into ½-inch dice
2 cups (16 fl oz) chicken stock
salt and freshly ground pepper
1 cup (8 fl oz) heavy cream
2–3 tablespoons Madeira wine, preferably imported
freshly grated nutmeg
2 oz Brie cheese, rind removed and sliced into 8–12 thin pieces
chopped fresh basil

CLEAN THE MUSHROOMS by brushing off any dirt with a dry towel or mushroom brush. Chop coarsely and set aside.

IN A SAUTÉ PAN or large saucepan over medium-low heat, melt the butter. When hot, add the shallot and onion and sauté, stirring occasionally, until translucent, 7–10 minutes. Add the mushrooms, raise the heat to medium and sauté, stirring, until the mushrooms are tender and begin to release their liquid, 8–10 minutes; do not allow the onion to brown. Add the potato, stock and salt to taste, cover partially and simmer until the mushrooms and potato are soft, 15–20 minutes, adjusting the heat if necessary to maintain a simmer.

REMOVE FROM THE HEAT and let cool slightly. Working in batches, process in a food processor fitted with the metal blade or in a blender until a smooth purée forms. Return the purée to the saucepan and add the cream. Place over medium-low heat and bring almost to a simmer; do not allow to boil. Add the Madeira to taste, a little nutmeg and a little pepper. Taste and adjust the seasonings.

LADLE INTO WARMED SOUP BOWLS. Float 2 or 3 pieces of the cheese on the surface, then sprinkle with basil and serve. ❧

Sardine Butter

If you like, spread this quickly made, aromatic butter onto fresh, hot toast and serve as an hors d'oeuvre before or a companion to the mushroom soup at right.

Drain the oil from 2 cans (4 oz each) skinless, boneless Portuguese sardines. Using a fork, combine the sardines with ¹/₂ cup (4 oz) unsalted butter, at room temperature, mashing to a paste. Season lightly with lemon juice and cayenne pepper. Chill overnight. Serve with rounds of crisp brown toast.

TOMATO SOUP

SERVES 4

Although at first glance this recipe might look like a standard cream of tomato soup, there is something both classic and new about it. The classic element is the use of a potato, which gives the soup thick body without detracting from the flavor of the tomatoes. The sour cream stirred in at the end strikes me as an innovative touch. If you like a hint of spice, feel free to add the cayenne pepper.

2 lb ripe tomatoes, peeled, seeded (see page 70) and chopped
1 white potato, peeled and diced
2 teaspoons sugar
1 teaspoon salt
1 teaspoon freshly ground black pepper
leaves from 2 fresh basil sprigs
1 cup (8 fl oz) chicken stock
½ cup (4 fl oz) sour cream
⅛ teaspoon cayenne pepper, optional
chopped fresh parsley

IN A LARGE SAUCEPAN over low heat, combine the tomatoes, potato, sugar, salt, black pepper and basil. Stir to mix, cover and cook, stirring often, until the potato is tender, about 20 minutes. Add the stock and cook for another 2–3 minutes. Remove from the heat and pass through a food mill or sieve placed over a clean saucepan.

PLACE OVER MEDIUM-LOW HEAT and reheat to serving temperature. Just before serving, in a small bowl, combine 1 cup of the tomato mixture with the sour cream. Stir until smooth and then stir back into the rest of the soup. Taste and adjust the seasonings, adding the cayenne pepper, if using. Ladle into warmed bowls and garnish with parsley. Serve very hot. ✤

CAESAR CARDINI

Caesar salad takes its name from the man who invented it, Caesar Cardini, an Italian chef in the Mexican border town of Tijuana, Baja California. In 1924, during Tijuana's heyday as a popular weekend getaway for stars and moguls from the growing movie business in Hollywood, Cardini reputedly created the salad as an impromptu late-night snack for Fourth of July revelers. The salad quickly became a hit and spread to fashionable restaurants north of the border.

CAESAR SALAD

SERVES 4

The Caesar salad enjoyed a major resurgence in popularity in the late 1980s, and the trend has continued to this day, with almost every restaurant offering one on its menu. This modern version addresses the health concerns a lot of people have about the traditional method of enriching the dressing with a coddled egg. I use plain yogurt instead— low fat or nonfat works fine—and it gives the dressing a wonderfully tangy, creamy quality that everyone who has tasted it loves.

1 large or 2 small heads romaine lettuce, preferably with
  small leaves
3 or 4 slices French or Italian bread, each ½ inch thick
3 tablespoons extra-virgin olive oil, plus ½ cup (4 fl oz)
  extra-virgin olive oil
2 cloves garlic
salt
6–8 anchovy fillets in olive oil, drained
1½ teaspoons dry mustard
2 tablespoons fresh lemon juice
1½ tablespoons plain yogurt
½ cup (2 oz) freshly grated Parmesan cheese
freshly ground pepper

DISCARD ANY TOUGH or discolored outer leaves from the lettuce head(s). Separate the leaves and reserve the large ones for another use. Rinse the smaller inner leaves and dry thoroughly. Break the leaves into halves or thirds. Place in a salad bowl, cover with a damp kitchen towel and refrigerate for 20–30 minutes to crisp.

REMOVE THE CRUSTS from the bread slices and discard. Cut the bread into ½-inch cubes. You should have about 2 cups.

IN A LARGE FRYING PAN over low heat, warm the 3 tablespoons olive oil. Meanwhile, using the flat side of a chopping knife, smash 1 of the garlic cloves. When the oil is hot, add the garlic to the pan and sauté for 1–2 minutes. Add the bread cubes and fry, stirring and tossing, until crisp and golden on all sides, 4–5 minutes. Discard the garlic. Sprinkle the bread cubes with a little salt. Using a slotted spoon, transfer to paper towels to drain. Set the croutons aside to cool.

CHOP THE REMAINING GARLIC CLOVE and combine with the ½ cup olive oil in a blender. Purée until smooth. In a small bowl, and using a fork, mash the anchovies until they form a paste. Add to the oil and garlic in the blender along with the mustard, lemon juice and yogurt. Blend at high speed until a smooth emulsion forms. Add 2 tablespoons of the Parmesan cheese and blend again. Season with a little salt, remembering that anchovies are salty, and a little pepper.

ADD THREE-FOURTHS OF THE DRESSING to the lettuce and toss to coat well. Add about half of the remaining cheese and toss again. Add more dressing or more seasonings to taste. Sprinkle with the croutons and the remaining cheese. Serve immediately. ⚜

JOSE WILSON

For many years, José Wilson, who lived in Rockport, Massachusetts, and was a great cook in her own right, served as James Beard's right-hand woman, helping him write his many articles, columns and books. This is how Jim paid simple, eloquent tribute to her in the introduction to his book *The New James Beard* (1981): "Not only was she a wonderful collaborator but she was a beloved friend. Her untimely death is a great loss to me, and I consider this book a monument to her memory."

JOSE WILSON'S FILLET OF SOLE ROCKPORT

SERVES 4

Given to me by the late José (pronounced Josie) Wilson, this recipe anticipates how confident we would become by the late 1980s with all the different culinary influences we'd absorbed in the previous decades. Its combination of flavors reflects that fact: each highly distinctive, yet all of them nicely balanced to complement the delicate sole fillets.

¼ cup (2 oz) unsalted butter
¼ cup (2 oz) Dijon mustard
2 tablespoons prepared horseradish
¼ cup (2 fl oz) fresh lemon juice
4 tablespoons (1 oz) freshly grated Parmesan cheese
½ cup (4 fl oz) sour cream
4 sole fillets, 6–8 oz each

PREHEAT A BROILER. Butter a flameproof gratin dish in which the fillets will fit comfortably in a single layer.

IN A SAUCEPAN over medium-low heat, melt the butter. Remove from the heat and stir in the mustard, horseradish, lemon juice, 2 tablespoons of the Parmesan cheese and the sour cream. Taste and adjust as needed; the sauce should be thick and pungent.

PLACE THE SOLE FILLETS in the prepared dish and spread the mustard sauce thickly on the fillets. Sprinkle with the remaining 2 tablespoons Parmesan cheese. Place under the broiler about 4 inches from the heat and broil until the sauce is lightly browned and glazed and the fish is opaque throughout when pierced with the tip of a knife, about 5 minutes; do not overcook. Transfer to warmed individual plates and serve at once. ♕

ROAST RACK OF LAMB

SERVES 4–6

Americans' growing knowledge of French and Italian cooking over the last four decades is responsible for the appearance of rack of lamb on the menu of nearly every good restaurant today. What I like about this recipe is how simple it is, with none of the fussing about with smearings of mustard or coatings of bread crumbs that you find in so many lamb recipes. Serve it for a special dinner party.

2 center-cut racks of lamb, 6 ribs each
1 clove garlic, cut in half
2 tablespoons finely chopped fresh rosemary, plus sprigs
  for garnish
salt and freshly ground pepper

PREHEAT AN OVEN to 450°F. Trim the lamb racks of any excess fat, leaving only a very thin layer of fat. Rub the racks generously with the garlic halves and coat the fat and flesh sides with the chopped rosemary, pressing it in firmly with your fingers. Season to taste with salt and pepper.

PLACE THE LAMB on a flat rack in a roasting pan, fat side down, and roast for 15 minutes. Turn the lamb fat side up, reduce the heat to 400°F and roast until the meat springs back when touched with a finger, or until an instant-read thermometer inserted into the thickest part of the meat away from the bone registers 125°F, 20–30 minutes for medium-rare. Alternatively, using a sharp knife, cut into the meat; it should be medium pink.

TRANSFER THE LAMB to a warmed serving plate and carve into chops. Serve immediately on warmed individual plates, with some of the platter juices spooned over the chops. Garnish with the rosemary sprigs. ☙

Braised Pork Chops

A very basic French country-style braise gets a touch of elegance from the addition to its pan juices of a little Dijon mustard.

Melt 2 tablespoons unsalted butter in a frying pan. Add 2 pork chops (1½ inches thick) and brown on both sides. Transfer to a braising pan. Sauté 1 onion and 1 celery stalk, both thinly sliced, in the same frying pan, then add ½ cup (4 fl oz) each dry white wine and water. Bring to a boil and pour over the chops. Season with salt, cover and braise in a 300°F oven until tender, 1½–2 hours. Remove the chops. Strain the pan juices and combine with 2 tablespoons Dijon mustard and 2 teaspoons capers. Simmer for a few minutes and pour over the chops. Serves 2.

"Eternity is two people
and a roast turkey."

—James Dent

ROAST TURKEY

SERVES 6–8

Turkey has always been a part of the American table, but I include this recipe for two important reasons. First, it marks the fact that, after years of eating frozen turkeys, Americans have reached a point at which it is once again possible to buy fresh farm-raised turkeys. The other reason is that, in the fast-paced world of the 1990s, there are a lot of people who don't know how to roast a turkey. I can promise you these instructions work. Accompany the bird with the gravy included in the recipe and with the baked chestnut and sausage dressing (page 146), the apple-orange cranberry sauce (page 147) and the mashed potatoes and parsnips (page 162) that follow.

1 fresh turkey, 10–12 lb
½ lemon
1 yellow onion, quartered
2 celery stalks, cut into 2-inch lengths
2 or 3 fresh thyme sprigs
1 bay leaf
3 or 4 fresh parsley sprigs
salt and freshly ground pepper
¼ cup (2 oz) unsalted butter, melted
1 cup water

FOR THE GRAVY:
1 cup water
3 tablespoons unsalted butter
3 tablespoons all-purpose flour
2 cups (16 fl oz) chicken stock
2 tablespoons dry sherry

REMOVE THE TURKEY from the refrigerator about 1 hour before roasting to allow it to come to room temperature (figure on a total roasting time of 2½–3 hours). Remove the neck, gizzard and so forth from the cavity and discard. Rinse the turkey inside and out and dry with paper towels.

POSITION A RACK in the lower third of an oven and preheat to 425°F. Oil a roasting rack and place in a roasting pan; set aside. Remove any excess fat from around the body cavity of the turkey and rub the inside with the lemon half. Leave the lemon half inside the cavity. Add the onion, celery, thyme, bay leaf, parsley and a little salt to the cavity and fasten closed with a small skewer.

TRUSS THE TURKEY so that it is easier to handle when roasting, securing the legs close to the body with kitchen string. Brush the outside with some of the melted butter and sprinkle with salt and pepper. Place breast-side down in the prepared rack and add the water to the pan. Place in the oven and roast for 30 minutes. Carefully turn the turkey breast side up, reduce the heat to 325°F and continue to roast, basting with the remaining melted butter or pan juices every 25–30 minutes, until the turkey is browned, or until an instant-read thermometer inserted into the breast away from the bone registers 165°F and into the thigh registers 180°F, 2–2½ hours more. Transfer the turkey to a warmed platter, cover loosely with aluminum foil and let rest for 15–20 minutes.

TO MAKE THE GRAVY, skim the fat from the pan juices, add the 1 cup water and place over medium heat. Bring to a boil and boil for 2–3 minutes, stirring with a wooden spoon to dislodge any browned bits stuck to the bottom of the pan. Strain into a bowl and set aside. In a saucepan over medium heat, melt the 3 tablespoons of butter. Add the flour and stir rapidly for a few seconds to cook the flour. Add the strained pan juices and the chicken stock. Cook, stirring rapidly, until smooth and thickened, 1–2 minutes. Stir in the sherry, then season to taste with salt and pepper. Pour into a warmed sauceboat. Carve the turkey (see right) and serve with gravy.

CARVING A TURKEY

To carve a turkey, you need a good, sharp slicing knife with a long, flexible but sturdy blade and a two-pronged carving fork to help steady the bird. Follow these three steps, carving one side of the turkey completely before starting the other side:

1. *Remove the leg and wing.* Place the turkey breast up on a carving board. Cut through the skin between the thigh and breast. Move the leg to locate the thigh joint, then cut through the joint to sever the leg from the body. In the same way, remove the wing, cutting through the shoulder joint where it meets the breast.

2. *Separate the drumstick and thigh.* Cut through the joint between the drumstick and thigh to separate them. Serve them whole. Or carve them, cutting off the meat parallel to the bone in thin slices.

3. *Carve the breast.* Just above the thigh and shoulder joints, carve a deep horizontal cut toward the rib cage, creating a base cut on one side of the breast. Starting near the breastbone and cutting downward and parallel to the rib cage, carve thin slices from the breast, ending at the base cut.

BAKED CHESTNUT AND SAUSAGE DRESSING

SERVES 6–8

I always prefer to bake a dressing separately, rather than to stuff a turkey. Unstuffed, the turkey cooks faster, and a dressing does not absorb any of the fat from the bird. This recipe (photograph on page 144) was given to me by the chef in the kitchen of the Stanford Court Hotel on Nob Hill in San Francisco.

1 loaf French or Italian coarse country bread, 1 lb
3 tablespoons unsalted butter
1½ cups (6 oz) chopped yellow onion
½ cup (2½ oz) chopped celery (about 2 stalks)
½ lb well-seasoned lean bulk pork sausage
¼ lb lean ground beef
2–2½ cups (16–20 fl oz) milk, at room temperature
1 jar (1 lb) prepared roasted chestnuts, chopped
1 tablespoon chopped fresh sage
¼ cup chopped fresh parsley
salt and freshly ground pepper

THE NIGHT BEFORE you plan to serve the dressing, tear the bread into small pieces and spread out on a baking sheet. Let dry, uncovered.

THE NEXT DAY, preheat an oven to 375°F. Butter a 3-quart baking dish. In a frying pan over medium-low heat, melt the butter. When hot, add the onion and celery and sauté, stirring occasionally, until the onion is translucent, 7–10 minutes. Transfer to a plate and set aside. Add the sausage and beef to the same pan over medium heat and sauté, breaking them up with a fork, until the meats are crumbly and have changed color, 8–10 minutes; do not allow to brown. Remove from the heat, drain off any fat and set aside.

PLACE THE BREAD in a large bowl. While tossing the bread with a fork, drizzle the milk a little at a time, just until the bread cubes are evenly moistened. You may not need all of the milk. Add the reserved onion and celery and meat mixture along with the chestnuts, sage and parsley. Season to taste with salt and pepper and mix until well blended. Spoon loosely into the prepared baking dish. Bake, uncovered, until lightly browned on top, 50–60 minutes. Serve immediately directly from the dish. ♔

APPLE-ORANGE CRANBERRY SAUCE

MAKES 3¹/₂–4 CUPS; SERVES 6–8

In the beginning, at least in most of our lifetimes, was canned cranberry sauce. Then people started fancying the canned stuff up with a little grated orange zest or orange juice. Today, with both fresh and frozen whole cranberries widely available, more and more people are making their own cranberry sauces and adding all kinds of other fruits. I've seen some that include pears, oranges, even pineapple. This one with apple (photograph on page 144) is a favorite.

1 orange, preferably thin skinned
2 cups water
1 Granny Smith or other tart green apple, quartered, cored,
  peeled and chopped into small pieces
3 cups (12 oz) fresh cranberries
1¼ cups (10 oz) sugar
½ teaspoon ground cinnamon
¼ teaspoon ground cloves

CUT THE ORANGE in half and squeeze the juice from both halves into a bowl, discarding any seeds. Using a spoon, scoop out and discard the pulp and the white membrane from both halves. Cut the peels into small dice. Place in a small saucepan with the water and bring to a boil over high heat. Boil for 10 minutes to soften, then drain and set aside.

PLACE THE APPLE in a saucepan. Pick over the cranberries, discarding any soft ones, and add to the apple along with the diced orange peel, orange juice, sugar, cinnamon and cloves. Place over medium-high heat and bring to a boil. Reduce the heat to medium-low, cover partially and simmer gently until thickened, the apple is tender and the cranberries have burst, 10–15 minutes.

TRANSFER TO A BOWL and let cool before serving. The sauce can also be covered and refrigerated for up to 1 day; bring back to room temperature before serving. ♔

"There is a tendency nowadays to make a separation between an everyday cook and a so-called gourmet cook. And the simpler cooks seem to stand in awe. Unfortunately *gourmet* has become synonymous with *fancy* and it conjures up the kind of cook who gussies up dinner with rich sauces and goes in for fussy, overworked dishes. We'd all be better off today if we admitted that there is really no such thing as gourmet cooking—there is simply good cooking."

—Marion Cunningham,
The Fannie Farmer Cookbook
(1990)

"The Southwest offers me a wide variety of visual inspiration. The land itself, with its rich earth tones, is reflected in the colors of cornmeal, in pale-brown pinto beans sauces, in the brick red of dried chiles and the vivid green of cactus. The textures of Southwestern food add another visual dimension: the rough, blistered surfaces of tortillas, the chunky consistency of a fresh salsa, the ridged pattern of a dried corn husk etched on a tamale."

—John Sedlar, *Modern Southwest Cusine* (1986)

FAJITAS

SERVES 6

The Tex-Mex craze continued to grow in the late 1980s. One of the dishes that became synonymous with the trend was fajitas, a clever use for skirt-steak trimmings that, depending on which account you read, developed years ago around San Antonio or in the border towns on either side of the Rio Grande. Soon every Tex-Mex, Southwest or Mexican restaurant was offering sizzling platters of meat, onions and peppers. Some even featured versions with chicken breast strips or whole shrimp.

2 lb skirt steak or flank steak
¼ cup (2 fl oz) fresh lime juice
¼ cup (2 fl oz) vegetable oil
½ teaspoon ground cumin
½ teaspoon dried oregano
2 cloves garlic, finely chopped
2 tablespoons olive oil
2 sweet red onions, sliced
2 red bell peppers, seeded, deribbed and sliced lengthwise
  into strips ¼ inch wide
salt and freshly ground pepper
12–18 flour or corn tortillas

1 cup (8 fl oz) sour cream
fresh tomato salsa (recipe on page 150)
guacamole (recipe on page 151)

TRIM THE MEAT of any excess fat and slice against the grain into thin strips about ½ inch wide. Place the strips in a shallow nonaluminum dish. In a bowl, stir together the lime juice, vegetable oil, cumin, oregano and garlic. Pour over the meat strips and turn the strips several times to coat them evenly with the marinade. Cover and refrigerate for 2–3 hours, turning the meat strips occasionally.

IN A LARGE SAUTÉ PAN or frying pan over medium heat, warm the olive oil. When hot, add the onions and bell peppers and sauté, tossing occasionally, until the onions are translucent and the peppers are soft, 6–8 minutes. Transfer to a large warmed plate and keep warm.

PLACE A LARGE, HEAVY FRYING PAN or griddle over medium-high heat. When hot, working in batches, place some of the beef strips in the pan or on the griddle, season to taste with salt and pepper and cook quickly, turning once, until well browned and done to your liking, about 2 minutes total for medium-rare. Transfer to the plate holding the onions and peppers.

IN THE SAME PAN or griddle over medium heat, warm the tortillas, turning once, about 10 seconds on each side. Alternatively, wrap the tortillas in aluminum foil and warm in a 250°F oven for a few minutes.

TO SERVE, place some meat on a warm tortilla and add some onion slices and pepper strips, sour cream, salsa and guacamole. Fold the tortilla in half and eat out of hand. ⚜

NONALUMINUM DISHES AND COOKWARE

Recipes that call for acidic ingredients (citrus juice, tomatoes, vinegar or wine), egg yolks or some vegetables such as artichokes and asparagus should specify nonaluminum dishes or cookware. This is because the yolks or vegetables cause oxidation that discolors aluminum, and acidic foods produce a chemical reaction that results in their having an off taste and color. For these reasons, always use glass, ceramic or porcelain dishes, and cookware of stainless steel, enameled cast iron or steel, or tinned copper. Alternatively, use pots and pans made from anodized aluminum, which has been subjected to an electrolytic process that seals its natural surface pores, forming a tough, smooth surface that will not react with food.

FRESH TOMATO SALSA

MAKES ABOUT 2¹/₂ CUPS

Fresh salsa (photograph on page 148) is the ketchup of the 1990s. You'll find clear plastic tubs of it in the refrigerator cases of most good-sized markets, although it is easy to make at home.

1 lb ripe tomatoes, finely chopped
¾ cup (3 oz) chopped sweet red onion
4 fresh serrano chili peppers, seeded and finely chopped
1 tablespoon finely chopped fresh cilantro
salt
2–3 teaspoons fresh lime juice

IN A BOWL, combine the tomatoes, onion, chili peppers, cilantro and salt to taste. Then stir in the lime juice to taste. Taste and adjust the seasonings. Cover and let stand for 30–40 minutes to allow the flavors to blend.

GUACAMOLE

MAKES ABOUT 2 CUPS

You've got to serve your fajitas with guacamole (photograph page 148), an avocado dip that became popular nationwide in the late 1980s and early 1990s. That isn't to say there is anything new about guacamole. It had been a specialty of California for decades, and had prominent mention in the first definitive book on the cooking of California, written in 1952 by Helen Evans Brown, who pioneered California cuisine.

2 ripe avocados
1 tablespoon finely chopped green onion, including some
   of the tender green top
1 fresh serrano chili pepper, seeded, if desired, and finely chopped
1 large ripe tomato, peeled, seeded (see page 70) and
   finely chopped
1 tablespoon finely chopped fresh cilantro, plus sprigs for garnish
1 tablespoon fresh lime juice, or more to taste
salt

WORKING WITH 1 AVOCADO at a time, cut in half, remove the pit and, using a spoon, scoop out the flesh into a bowl. Using a fork, break up the avocado flesh lightly and evenly. Do not reduce to a purée; the avocado should retain some texture.

ADD THE GREEN ONION, chili pepper, tomato, chopped cilantro and lime juice. Stir with a fork until well mixed. Season to taste with salt and add more lime juice, if necessary. Place in a serving bowl, garnish with the cilantro sprigs and serve immediately, as guacamole will gradually darken when exposed to the air. ♕

"Here is our favorite dip, another Mexican contribution. I recently saw it spelled, phonetically, 'waca molay,' but not, I assure you, in a West Coast publication."

—Helen Evans Brown,
West Coast Cookbook (1952)

"The art of cooking produces the dishes, but it is the art of eating that transforms them into a meal."

—Marcella Hazan

ITALIAN COUNTRY PIZZA

MAKES TWO 10- TO 12-INCH PIZZAS; SERVES 2–4

With the rise of specialty pizzerias like those of Wolfgang Puck or the California Pizza Kitchen chain, more and more people are trying their hands at making pizza at home. This recipe for an authentic, rustic Italian pie is a good way to start. It does not call for a pizza brick or ceramic baking tiles, although either will help you achieve an even crisper, higher-rising crust.

1 package (2½ teaspoons) active dry yeast
1½ cups lukewarm water (110°F)
4 cups (1¼ lb) all-purpose flour
2 teaspoons salt
¼ cup (2 fl oz) olive oil, plus extra olive oil for brushing
yellow cornmeal
2 lb ripe tomatoes, peeled, seeded (see page 70) and
   coarsely chopped
16 anchovy fillets in olive oil, drained
4 cloves garlic, minced
2 teaspoons minced fresh oregano or 1 teaspoon dried oregano
salt and freshly ground pepper
1 lb mozzarella cheese, thinly sliced

IN A SMALL BOWL, dissolve the yeast in ¼ cup of the lukewarm water and set aside until foamy, about 3 minutes. In a large bowl, stir together the flour and salt with a wooden spoon. Add the yeast mixture, the remaining 1¼ cups water and the ¼ cup olive oil. Mix thoroughly with the wooden spoon until the ingredients come together to form a dough. With your hands, gather together the dough and place on a floured work surface. Knead until smooth, satiny and no longer sticky, about 10 minutes, adding more flour or water as necessary. Place in a warmed bowl, cover the bowl in plastic wrap and let the dough rise in a warm place until doubled in bulk, 45–60 minutes.

PREHEAT AN OVEN to 450°F. Lightly sprinkle 2 baking sheets with cornmeal.

PUNCH DOWN THE DOUGH and divide into 2 equal pieces. On a floured work surface, flatten or roll out each piece into a round 10–12 inches in diameter. Place each round on a prepared baking sheet, cover with a kitchen towel and let rise for 20 minutes.

USING YOUR FINGERTIPS, make an overall pattern of indentations over the surface of each dough round, then brush the rounds with olive oil. Spoon the tomatoes over the 2 rounds, dividing them evenly. Then, using the back of the spoon, spread to within ½ inch of the rim of each round. Arrange the anchovy fillets on top and sprinkle with the garlic, oregano and salt and pepper to taste. Top with the mozzarella cheese and brush with olive oil.

BAKE UNTIL THE EDGES of the crusts are golden and the tops are bubbly, 15–20 minutes. Cut and serve immediately. ♛

Pizza Variations

If you wish, half of the dough for this pizza can be wrapped in plastic, refrigerated and prepared and baked separately, or frozen for up to 1 month. The dough can also be divided and made into smaller pizzas. Additional toppings can be arranged on the tomatoes, including artichoke hearts and black olives; onion rings and green olives; or sliced cooked sausages and roasted yellow bell pepper strips.

"To achieve pasta nirvana, much attention to detail needs to be paid. Then you'll understand why after Americans visit Italy, they come back babbling about a simple little fresh pasta with peas, butter, and cheese. But what noodles! What peas! What butter! What cheese! They all were the best quality and were cooked perfectly. Not a complicated recipe but one that required finesse. Artless and artful."

—Joyce Goldstein, *Kitchen Conversations* (1996)

LINGUINE WITH PESTO

SERVES 6

Many factors made linguine with pesto a ubiquitous dish in the late 1980s. Every cook who had a backyard or sunny windowsill, it seemed, was growing fresh basil, or finding it fairly easily in food shops, produce shops and/or farmers' markets. Grated Parmesan cheese in cardboard tubes had already been forsaken, with freshly grated replacing it. Pine nuts had also become widespread, and extra-virgin olive oil was in everyone's cupboard. Finally, either a food processor or blender, which make good pesto sauce in a matter of seconds, stood on a countertop in the kitchens of most American cooks.

1 cup firmly packed fresh basil leaves
2 cloves garlic, chopped
¼ cup (1¼ oz) pine nuts
salt
¼ cup (1 oz) freshly grated Parmesan cheese, preferably Italian,
  plus extra for the table
¼–⅓ cup (2–3 fl oz) extra-virgin olive oil
1 lb dried linguine

BRING A LARGE POT three-fourths full of water to a rolling boil over high heat.

MEANWHILE, place the basil in a food processor fitted with the metal blade or in a blender. Pulse a few times until the leaves are finely chopped. Add the garlic, pine nuts and ¼ teaspoon salt and pulse a few more times. Add the ¼ cup Parmesan cheese and again pulse until well blended and smooth. While continuing to pulse, gradually add enough of the oil to form a smooth, creamy sauce. Taste and adjust with more salt, if necessary. Set aside.

ADD 1 TABLESPOON SALT and the pasta to the boiling water and stir a few times to separate the pasta and keep it from sticking to the bottom of the pot. Cook, stirring once or twice, until al dente (tender but still firm to the bite), 8–10 minutes or according to the package directions.

SCOOP OUT AND RESERVE about ½ cup of the pasta water. Then drain the pasta and transfer to a warmed serving bowl. Add the basil mixture and toss well, adding a little of the pasta water if needed for the sauce to coat the pasta noodles evenly. Serve immediately. Pass Parmesan cheese at the table. ♛

"If the definition of poetry allowed that it could be composed with the products of the field as well as with words, *pesto* would be in every anthology."

—Marcella Hazan

FETTUCCINE WITH PROSCIUTTO AND PEAS

SERVES 6

A delicate and flavorful creation for springtime, this easy-to-assemble fresh pasta dish features prosciutto, the salt-cured raw ham of Parma that has become very popular in recent years. It can be found in virtually any Italian delicatessen, specialty-food store or upscale market.

2 tablespoons unsalted butter
½ cup (2½ oz) finely chopped yellow onion
4–6 thin slices prosciutto, cut into narrow strips
1 cup (8 fl oz) heavy cream
salt to taste, plus 1 tablespoon
2 cups (10 oz) shelled peas
1 lb fettuccine, fresh (recipe on page 116) or dried
½ cup (2 oz) freshly grated Parmesan cheese, preferably Italian

BRING A LARGE POT three-fourths full of water to a rolling boil over high heat.

MEANWHILE, in a large sauté pan over medium-low heat, melt the butter. When hot, add the onion and sauté until translucent, 7–10 minutes. Add the prosciutto and cream and simmer, stirring, 3–4 minutes longer. Season to taste with salt and set aside; keep warm.

ADD THE 1 TABLESPOON SALT, the peas and the pasta to the boiling water and stir a few times to separate the pasta and to keep it from sticking to the bottom of the pot. Cook, stirring once or twice, until al dente (tender but still firm to the bite), 12–15 seconds for fresh pasta or 8–10 minutes for dried, or according to the package directions.

DRAIN IMMEDIATELY and add to the cream mixture in the sauté pan over high heat. Toss well and cook briefly until well blended and hot. Transfer to a warmed serving bowl or individual plates and serve immediately. Pass the Parmesan cheese at the table. ♕

POLENTA WITH PARMESAN CHEESE

MAKES ABOUT 8 CUPS; SERVES 4–6

Boiled, baked or fried, this northern Italian cornmeal porridge has become a favorite staple of American cooks. This simple version of the dish is enriched with butter and Parmesan cheese. Be sure to use regular long-cooking polenta rather than the quick-cooking variety. Serve in place of rice or noodles with a pot-roasted, braised, stewed or sautéed dish that has lots of flavorful sauce.

7 cups water
2 teaspoons salt
2 cups (12 oz) long-cooking Italian polenta
¼ cup (2 oz) unsalted butter, cut into small cubes
1 cup (4 oz) freshly grated Parmesan cheese, preferably Italian

IN A DEEP, HEAVY SAUCEPAN over high heat, bring the water to a rapid boil and add the salt. While stirring continuously with a long-handled wooden spoon, gradually add the polenta in a thin, steady stream until all of it has been incorporated. Continue to stir constantly to keep lumps from forming and reduce the heat until the mixture only bubbles occasionally. Cook, stirring, until thick, smooth and creamy, 20–25 minutes. Regularly scrape the bottom and sides of the pan to avoid sticking or lumping. The polenta is ready when it starts to come away from the sides of the pan and the spoon stands upright unaided.

REMOVE FROM THE HEAT and stir in the butter, a few cubes at a time, until fully absorbed. Then stir in ½ cup (2 oz) of the Parmesan cheese. Return the pan to the heat for a few seconds, continuing to stir, until the polenta is piping hot.

TRANSFER TO A WARMED BOWL or platter and serve immediately. Pass the remaining ½ cup Parmesan cheese at the table. ☙

NOTES ON POLENTA

A staple of the ancient Roman legions, who were known to mutiny if the grain supply ran out and they had to make do with mere meat, polenta is a kind of porridge that is served with a savory sauce, or with butter and grated cheese. It takes the place of pasta, rice or potatoes and sometimes even bread. Made today from cornmeal—in classical times Romans used wheat or millet—polenta can be served immediately after cooking, or it can be patted into a big cake, allowed to cool, sliced and then later baked or fried. In Italy today, the best polenta comes from cornmeal that is freshly ground during the two- to three-week harvest period. The long-cooking imported variety has a fine, even grind, and cooks to a smoother, more even consistency than American cornmeal or quick-cooking Italian polenta.

SPINACH RISOTTO

SERVES 6–8

½ lb spinach
6 tablespoons (3 oz) unsalted butter
2 cups (14 oz) Arborio rice
½ cup (4 fl oz) dry white wine
4½ cups (36 fl oz) chicken stock
salt and freshly ground pepper
½ cup (2 oz) freshly grated Parmesan cheese, preferably Italian

Starting in the late 1980s, risotto, a creamy rice dish that has been a staple in northern Italy since the 17th century, became a featured item on most Italian restaurant menus in the United States. For a true risotto, you must use Italian Arborio, Carnaroli or Vialone Nano rice, a short-grained, starchy variety that gives the risotto its rich character and chewy texture.

REMOVE THE STEMS from the spinach leaves, discarding any tough leaves as well. Rinse thoroughly and place in a saucepan with water still clinging to the leaves. Cover and place over medium heat until just wilted, about 1 minute. Drain well, pressing any liquid from the leaves. Chop coarsely and set aside. In a large saucepan over medium-low heat, melt 4 tablespoons of the butter. Add the rice and stir until coated with the butter, about 2 minutes. In another saucepan, combine the wine and stock and bring to a simmer. Reduce the heat under the rice to low. Stirring continuously, begin adding the hot liquid to the rice a ladleful at a time. Stirring often, let the rice absorb the liquid before adding more.

WHEN ALL OF THE LIQUID is absorbed, the kernels are tender but still firm at the center and the rice is creamy and smooth, the risotto is ready. Total cooking time should be about 20 minutes. If the rice is too firm, add more hot stock or water and cook a little longer. Then stir in the remaining 2 tablespoons butter and the chopped spinach. Season to taste with salt and pepper. Spoon into warmed individual bowls and top with the cheese. Serve immediately. ☙

BASMATI RICE WITH CASHEWS AND RAISINS

SERVES 4–6

1 cup (7 oz) basmati rice
1¾ cups water
¾ teaspoon salt
½ teaspoon ground turmeric
2 tablespoons unsalted butter
¼ cup (1 oz) diced yellow onion
¼ cup (1½ oz) golden raisins
¼ cup (1¼ oz) roasted cashews
1 teaspoon ground cardamom
⅓ cup (3 fl oz) unsweetened coconut milk

PLACE THE RICE in a sieve and rinse under cold running water; set aside to drain. In a heavy saucepan over high heat, combine the water, salt and turmeric and bring to a boil. Gradually add the rice while stirring constantly. When all of the rice is in the pan, reduce the heat to low, cover and cook slowly until the liquid is absorbed and the rice is tender, about 15 minutes.

MEANWHILE, melt the butter in a sauté pan over medium heat. When hot, add the onion and sauté until translucent, 2–3 minutes. Add the raisins, cashews and cardamom and cook for another 2 minutes. Stir in the coconut milk and cook for another 2 minutes.

WHEN THE RICE IS READY, remove from the heat and fluff with a fork. Add the onion-raisin mixture and toss gently with the fork until mixed. Taste and adjust the seasonings, then spoon into a warmed serving bowl and serve immediately. ☙

Chinese Spinach

Heat 2 teaspoons vegetable oil in a wok. Add 2 lb spinach, rinsed and drained, and 2 teaspoons salt and stir and toss for 2 minutes. Add 3 tablespoons soy sauce and cook for 1 minute longer. Serve at once. Serves 4–6.

PAELLA

SERVES 6

I believe that paella, the national rice dish of Spain, enjoyed a comeback lately as a result of the growing interest in risotto. Thanks to greater travel in Spain and to cookbooks like The Foods and Wines of Spain *by Penelope Casas, Americans have realized that you can make an authentic paella fairly easily, and without throwing in everything but the kitchen sink. In fact, the best paella I ever ate was in a little place north of Barcelona where I once stopped with our Spanish buying agent. It consisted of rice, pungent seasonings and a sauce made from sun-ripened tomatoes, cooked in a layer no more than an inch thick in a huge paella pan. The result was similar to the* socarrat *described by Penelope Casas in the excerpt at right.*

2 red bell peppers
½ lb medium-sized shrimp, peeled and deveined
1 tablespoon fresh lemon juice
4–5 tablespoons (2–2½ fl oz) olive oil
6 chicken pieces such as thighs, legs or halved breasts, 2 lb total
    weight, skinned and trimmed of excess fat
salt
1 yellow onion, chopped
2 cloves garlic, chopped
¼ lb cooked ham, diced
2 cups (14 oz) short-grain white rice (preferably Spanish
    or Italian Arborio)
2 large tomatoes, peeled, seeded (see page 70) and chopped
3½ cups (28 fl oz) chicken stock
½ cup (4 fl oz) dry white vermouth
pinch of saffron threads, optional
1 cup (5 oz) shelled peas
freshly ground pepper
chopped fresh parsley

PREHEAT A BROILER. Cut the bell peppers lengthwise into quarters and remove the stems, seeds and ribs. Place cut side down on a baking sheet and place under the broiler about 4 inches from the heat. Broil until the skins are blackened and blistered. Remove from the broiler and cover with aluminum foil. Let stand for 5–10 minutes to cool, then, using your fingers or a small knife, peel off the blackened skin. Cut the peppers into small pieces.

IN A BOWL, combine the shrimp and lemon juice and toss to coat evenly. Preheat an oven to 350°F.

IN A PAELLA PAN or in a wide, shallow ovenproof frying pan over medium-high heat, warm 4 tablespoons of the olive oil. Season the chicken pieces with salt and add to the hot oil. Sauté, turning as necessary, until golden on all sides, about 10 minutes total. Transfer to a plate and set aside.

ADD THE ONION, garlic and ham to the pan, adding the remaining 1 tablespoon olive oil if necessary, and sauté until the onion is translucent, 3–5 minutes. Add the shrimp and cook, stirring, until barely pink, about 2 minutes. Transfer the shrimp to the plate holding the chicken and reserve. Add the rice and stir until the kernels are coated with the oil, about 2 minutes. Add the tomatoes and roasted peppers and cook, stirring, for 2 minutes longer.

MEANWHILE, combine the stock and vermouth in a saucepan and bring to a boil, adding the saffron, if using. Add the peas to the rice, and carefully stir in the boiling stock mixture. Season to taste with salt and pepper and cook, uncovered, over medium heat, stirring occasionally, for 8 minutes. Part of the liquid should be absorbed, but the mixture should not be dry. Taste and adjust the seasonings.

ARRANGE THE SHRIMP and chicken pieces evenly atop the rice, then bury the shrimp and push the chicken halfway under. Place in the oven and bake, uncovered, until the rice is tender but still a little firm at the center, 15–20 minutes.

REMOVE FROM THE OVEN, cover loosely with aluminum foil and let stand for 5 minutes. Garnish with parsley and serve at once. ♨

"Ask a Spaniard what makes a perfect *paella* and never expect two opinions to coincide. The arguments may become heated as one insists that meat and seafood should not be mixed, another asserts that the 'real' *paella* should contain only the 'original' ingredients of rice, snails, and green beans, and yet a third denies the existence of a decent *paella* that has not been cooked over a woodburning fire in the out-of-doors, a method that produces the *socarrat,* a golden crust of rice that forms on the bottom of the pan and is considered the most desirable part of the *paella.*"

—Penelope Casas, *The Foods and Wines of Spain* (1983)

MASHED POTATOES WITH PARSNIPS

SERVES 6

Adding parsnips gives mashed potatoes a richer flavor with a slight edge of sweetness. You can use a ricer to produce a perfectly smooth texture, or a potato masher, which results in a slightly more textured dish.

3 lb potatoes
2 parsnips, 6–8 oz each, peeled and cut crosswise into slices ½ inch thick
2 teaspoons salt, plus salt to taste
⅓–¾ cup (3–6 fl oz) milk, heated
freshly ground pepper
chopped fresh parsley

IF YOU WILL BE USING A POTATO MASHER, peel the potatoes and cut them into ½-inch chunks. If you will be using a ricer, cut the unpeeled potatoes into chunks. Put the potatoes and parsnips in a large, heavy saucepan and add water to cover by 1 inch. Add the 2 teaspoons salt, place over medium-high heat and bring to a boil. Reduce the heat to medium and boil until tender when pierced with a fork, 20–25 minutes.

DRAIN THE POTATOES and parsnips well. If you are using a potato masher, mash the potatoes and parsnips in the pan until all the lumps are gone. If you are using a ricer, position it over a bowl and force the potatoes and parsnips through it. Then return the mixture to the saucepan. In both cases, place the pan over low heat. Adding the milk a little at a time, beat it in with a wooden spoon until the mixture is smooth, fluffy and very hot. Add only as much milk as is needed to achieve a good consistency; the mixture should not be soupy. Season to taste with salt and pepper. (If you must hold the mixture for a while before serving, cover and keep warm. Then, just before serving, return the pan to low heat and beat with a wooden spoon until hot.)

SPOON INTO A WARMED SERVING DISH or onto individual plates, and top with chopped parsley. Serve immediately. 🌱

WHOLE KERNEL CORN BREAD

SERVES 6

Here's another old-fashioned recipe that is made up-to-date by adding corn kernels cut fresh from the cob to a standard corn bread batter. When you think about it, though, you can imagine farmhouse cooks doing the same thing during corn season a century or more ago. Out of season, drained canned corn kernels can be substituted.

2 ears of corn
2 tablespoons plus 1 teaspoon salt
1¼ cups (6½ oz) yellow cornmeal
¾ cup (4 oz) all-purpose flour
2 teaspoons sugar
1 tablespoon baking powder
2 eggs, beaten
1 cup (8 fl oz) milk
¼ cup (2 oz) unsalted butter, melted and cooled

PREHEAT AN OVEN to 425°F. Butter an 8-inch square baking pan.

BRING A LARGE SAUCEPAN three-fourths full of water to a boil. Remove the husks and silks from the ears of corn and add the corn to the boiling water along with the 2 tablespoons salt. Cook for 5 minutes, then drain and plunge the corn into cold water to cool. Again, drain the cooled ears. Using a sharp knife, and resting the stem end of an ear in a wide shallow bowl, cut the kernels from the ear of corn. Repeat with the second ear. You should have about 1¼ cups kernels.

IN A BOWL, stir together the cornmeal, flour, sugar, the 1 teaspoon salt and the baking powder. In another bowl, stir together the eggs, milk and melted butter. Using a wooden spoon, quickly fold the flour mixture into the milk mixture; do not overmix. Stir in the corn kernels just until evenly distributed. Pour into the prepared pan.

BAKE UNTIL GOLDEN BROWN and a toothpick inserted into the center comes out clean, 25–30 minutes. Remove from the oven and let cool for a few minutes, then cut into squares and serve hot.

Sour Cream Belgian Waffles

An American country favorite, waffles have experienced a tremendous resurgence in recent years, especially Belgian waffles. They were first introduced to America at the Belgian pavillion in the New York World's Fair in 1939. This recipe yields waffles with a tender crumb, crisp exterior and rich, tangy flavor.

Separate 3 eggs and beat the yolks in a bowl. Beat in ¾ cup (6 fl oz) milk; ½ cup (4 oz) unsalted butter, melted; and ¾ cup (6 fl oz) sour cream. Combine and sift together 1½ cups (7½ oz) all-purpose flour, 2 teaspoons baking powder, ½ teaspoon baking soda and 1 tablespoon sugar. Add the flour mixture to the egg yolk mixture and beat well. In a separate bowl, beat the egg whites until stiff and carefully fold into the batter. Bake in a preheated waffle iron following the manufacturer's instructions. Serve with toppings of choice. Makes 8 waffles.

CRANBERRY MUFFINS

MAKES 12 MUFFINS

The 1990s seem to be the decade of the muffin; they have become hugely popular in breakfast and lunch joints and homes alike. Today you can also find dried cherries and blueberries, which can be used in place of the cranberries in these muffins.

¾ cup (3 oz) dried cranberries, coarsely chopped
2 tablespoons Cointreau or other orange-flavored liqueur
2 cups (10 oz) all-purpose flour
1 tablespoon baking powder
½ teaspoon salt
¼ cup (2 oz) sugar
1 egg, lightly beaten, at room temperature
1 cup (8 fl oz) milk, at room temperature
¼ cup (2 oz) unsalted butter, melted

PREHEAT AN OVEN to 375°F. Butter 12 cups of a standard muffin tin(s). Place the cranberries in an ovenproof bowl and stir in the liqueur. Cover tightly with aluminum foil and place in the oven until the cranberries puff up and absorb the liquid, 5–10 minutes. In another bowl, sift together the flour, baking powder, salt and sugar.

In yet another bowl, whisk together the egg, milk and melted butter until well blended. Using a wooden spoon, quickly fold the flour mixture into the egg mixture, then stir in the cranberries; do not overmix. Spoon the batter into the prepared cups, filling them two-thirds full.

BAKE UNTIL WELL RISEN and browned and a toothpick inserted into the center comes out clean, 20–25 minutes. Remove from the oven and let stand in the tin(s) for about 3 minutes, then turn out onto a wire rack to cool. Serve warm or at room temperature. ✻

BRAN MUFFINS

MAKES 12 MUFFINS

1 cup (2½ oz) wheat bran
1 cup (5 oz) whole-wheat flour
¼ teaspoon salt
¼ cup (2 oz) firmly packed brown sugar
1½ teaspoons baking powder
1 teaspoon baking soda
½ cup (3 oz) golden raisins
½ cup (2 oz) walnuts, chopped
1 cup (8 fl oz) buttermilk, at room temperature
1 egg, lightly beaten, at room temperature
3 tablespoons dark molasses
¼ cup (2 oz) unsalted butter, melted

PREHEAT AN OVEN to 375°F. Butter 12 cups of a standard muffin tin(s). In a bowl, stir together the bran, flour, salt, sugar, baking powder, baking soda, raisins and walnuts. In another bowl, combine the buttermilk, egg, molasses and melted butter. Whisk until well blended. Using a few quick strokes, stir the buttermilk mixture into the flour mixture; do not overmix. Spoon the batter into the prepared cups, filling them two-thirds full.

BAKE UNTIL WELL RISEN and browned and a toothpick inserted into the center comes out clean, 20–25 minutes. Remove from the oven and let stand in the tin(s) for about 3 minutes, then turn out onto a wire rack to cool. Serve warm or at room temperature. ✻

A standard 12-cup muffin tin is commonly made of tin steel (shown here), aluminum or cast iron. It can also be used for cupcakes.

165

Apple Tart

Make pâte sucrée in a food processor: Using the metal blade, process together 2 cups (10 oz) all-purpose flour, 2/3 cup (5 oz) unsalted butter and 2 tablespoons sugar until the mixture resembles coarse bread crumbs.

With the motor running, add 1 egg yolk through the feed tube and only just enough cold water to bind the mixture into a ball.

Gather up the dough, roll out between sheets of plastic wrap and fit into a 10-inch black steel tart pan. Bake in a 400°F oven until golden brown, about 20 minutes. If the pastry puffs during baking, deflate with a knife tip.

Peel, core and slice 6–8 pippin apples and place in a saucepan with 1/2 cup (4 fl oz) orange juice. Simmer until just tender, 10–15 minutes. Drain and let cool. Paint the inside of the pastry case with sieved apricot jam, arrange the apple slices on the pastry, and glaze with more jam. Just before serving, sprinkle with sugar and put briefly under the broiler to get a caramel coating, which may burn in places. Serves 6–8.

GINGER APPLE CRISP

SERVES 6–8

The baking of homemade pies has steadily declined since mother went to work outside the home, but we have found a solution to the problem: crisps. We have been encouraging the recent pastry-shy generations to whip up fruit crisps. They are easy, with no pastry techniques required. Over the past decade we have succeeded in getting apple pie, disguised as a crisp, back on the table. Many pastry-shy cooks have even graduated into pastry experts. Stand aside grandma!

3 lb baking apples, peeled, quartered, cored and sliced
juice of 1 lemon
1 tablespoon cornstarch
1/3 cup (3 oz) granulated sugar
1/4 teaspoon ground ginger
1/8 teaspoon freshly grated nutmeg
1/2 cup (3 oz) chopped crystallized ginger
1 cup (5 oz) all-purpose flour
1/2 cup (3½ oz) firmly packed brown sugar
pinch of salt
6 tablespoons (3 oz) unsalted butter, chilled, cut into pieces
1/2 cup (2 oz) chopped walnuts

PREHEAT AN OVEN to 400°F.

PLACE THE APPLE SLICES in a large bowl and toss with the lemon juice. In another bowl, stir together the cornstarch, granulated sugar, ground ginger, nutmeg and crystallized ginger. Add to the apples and toss to coat evenly. Transfer to a 1½- or 2-quart pie dish, heaping the apples up in the center.

IN A BOWL, mix together the flour, brown sugar and salt. Drop in the butter and, using your fingertips, blend together until crumbly. Add the walnuts and toss and stir to combine. Sprinkle evenly over the apples.

BAKE UNTIL THE TOP IS BROWNED and the apples are tender, 45–50 minutes. Remove from the oven and serve warm or at room temperature. ⚜

Ginger Melon

As well as the dried and crystallized forms of ginger used in the recipe at left, you can also find wonderful stem ginger in syrup, which features in this quick little recipe.

Halve, seed, peel and cube a melon. Thinly slice 5 or 6 pieces stem ginger in syrup and add to the melon, together with some of the syrup. Add about 1 tablespoon lemon juice and stir gently to mix. Cover and chill for 1–2 hours before serving.

CREME BRULEE

SERVES 6

If there is one dessert that represents the 1990s it is crème brûlée *(burnt cream). This rich custard topped with a brittle layer of caramelized sugar has become a standard selection on the dessert menu of many good restaurants today. Some chefs and home cooks still caramelize the sugar the old-fashioned way, by heating a salamander—a heavy iron disk at the end of a long handle—over a stove burner until red hot, then holding it over the sugar. Other contemporary chefs have replaced their salamander with a small blowtorch! You can get the same results, though, by sliding the dessert under the broiler.*

3 cups (24 fl oz) heavy cream
6 egg yolks
2 tablespoons sugar
½ teaspoon vanilla extract
brown sugar

POUR THE CREAM into a saucepan over medium heat and heat until small bubbles appear around the edges of the pan. Set aside.

MEANWHILE, in a bowl, combine the egg yolks and sugar. Using a whisk or egg beater, beat until pale yellow and thick enough to fall from the whisk or beaters in a lazy ribbon, 3–5 minutes. Gradually add the cream to the yolk mixture while beating constantly.

POUR THE CREAM MIXTURE into a heatproof bowl or the top pan of a double boiler and set over (but not touching) simmering water in a saucepan or the bottom pan of the double boiler. Stir with a wooden spoon until the custard thickens and coats the back of a spoon, 5–10 minutes; do not allow to boil. Stir in the vanilla. Pour into six ½-cup flameproof ramekins, let cool, cover and chill thoroughly, about 2 hours.

JUST BEFORE SERVING, preheat a broiler. Sift a thin coating of brown sugar over the top of each custard, covering evenly. Place the sugar-topped custards on a baking sheet and slide under the broiler about 3 inches from the heat. The sugar will quickly melt and caramelize; watch carefully so the custards do not burn. Serve at once. ₩

VANILLA ICE CREAM

MAKES ABOUT 1 QUART; SERVES 6

The invasion of the electric gelato machine in Europe as well as America has resulted in the ice cream—, gelato- and sorbet-making craze of the 1980s and 1990s. This version of a classic vanilla frozen custard tastes best when made with a vanilla bean. If you like, after the bean has steeped in the cream and before you discard it, use a knife tip to scrape the tiny black vanilla seeds back into the cream. They'll give the finished ice cream an attractive speckled look that many people today know means you've a used real vanilla bean and not just extract.

2 cups (16 fl oz) light cream or half-and-half
1 piece vanilla bean, about 2 inches, slit halfway through
  lengthwise to expose the seeds, or 1 teaspoon vanilla extract
8 egg yolks
½ cup (4 oz) sugar
1 cup (8 fl oz) heavy cream

POUR THE LIGHT CREAM or half-and-half into a heavy saucepan and add the vanilla bean. (If you are using vanilla extract, you must add it later.) Place over low heat and heat until small bubbles appear around the edges of the pan. Remove from the heat and let cool for 5–10 minutes. Meanwhile, in a bowl, combine the egg yolks and sugar. Using a whisk or egg beaters, beat until pale yellow and thick enough to fall from the whisk or beaters in a lazy ribbon, 3–5 minutes.

DISCARD THE VANILLA BEAN, if using, and gradually pour the cream into the yolk mixture, beating constantly. Transfer to a heatproof bowl or the top pan of a double boiler placed over (but not touching) simmering water in a saucepan or the bottom pan of the double boiler. Cook, stirring constantly with a wooden spoon, until the custard thickens and lightly coats the back of the spoon, 5–10 minutes; do not allow to boil. Stir in the heavy cream and the vanilla extract, if using. Strain the custard through a fine-mesh sieve into a bowl and let cool to room temperature. Cover and chill well. Freeze in an ice cream maker according to the manufacturer's instructions. ⚜

Avocado Ice Cream

In a mixing bowl, stir together ³/₄ cup (6 oz) sugar and 2 cups (16 fl oz) half-and-half or milk until the sugar is dissolved. Halve, pit and peel 2 large, ripe avocados and press them through a sieve into another bowl. Stir the juice of 1 small lemon into the avocado purée, then stir in one-third of the half-and-half mixture and mix until smooth. Add the remaining half-and-half mixture and stir until smooth. Freeze in an ice cream maker according to the manufacturer's instructions. Makes about 1 quart.

Banana Ice Cream

Peel 4 bananas and cut into small pieces. In a food processor fitted with the metal blade or in a blender, purée the bananas quickly. Transfer to a bowl and add 1 cup (8 oz) sugar and the juice of ¹/₂ lemon and stir to mix well. Stir in 1¹/₂ cups (12 fl oz) milk and flavor with 2 or 3 tablespoons kirsch or rum. Freeze in an ice cream maker according to the manufacturer's instructions. Makes about 1 quart.

PINK GRAPEFRUIT GRANITA

SERVES 4–6

This recipe is an excellent example of how one trend in cooking can often lead to another related, simpler trend. No sooner had we all started enjoying homemade ice creams churned in the new generation of electric machines, the first of which originated in Italy, than we discovered granitas, the wonderful Italian frozen desserts that are easily made in a freezer tray or shallow stainless-steel bowl. Prepare this recipe the same day you plan to serve it. The granita will form a solid mass if you store it longer.

6 or 7 medium-sized pink grapefruits, preferably Texas Ruby
½ cup water
1 cup (8 oz) sugar
2 fresh mint sprigs, or as needed, plus extra sprigs for garnish
orange zest strips

BE SURE YOUR FREEZER is set at its coldest setting an hour before you begin to make the granita. Squeeze the juice from the grapefruit and strain through a fine-mesh sieve into a bowl. You will need 3–3½ cups juice. Cover and refrigerate until well chilled.

IN A SAUCEPAN over medium heat, combine the water and sugar. Bring to a boil, stirring to dissolve the sugar. Using a brush moistened with water, brush down the pan sides to remove any sugar crystals. Add the 2 mint sprigs and boil for 1 minute. Set aside until cool enough to taste, 5–10 minutes, then taste for flavor. If the syrup has a good mint flavor, remove and discard the mint; if not, add more mint and repeat the boiling and cooling. Set aside to cool completely.

WHEN THE SYRUP HAS COOLED, stir it into the chilled grapefruit juice until completely blended. Pour this mixture into a shallow stainless-steel bowl or other stainless-steel container. (Ice cube trays will work if you have nothing else at hand.) Place in the freezer.

AFTER ABOUT 20 MINUTES, check to see if any ice crystals have formed. If they have, stir to break them up with a fork. Continue to check every 15–20 minutes and stir as necessary to prevent the crystals from forming a solid mass, scraping the bottom and sides of the pan to break up the crystals each time. Frequent stirring is important to producing a uniformly textured granita. Under proper conditions, the granita will freeze in 1½–2 hours. If your freezer is not cold enough or is too full of food, however, it can take up to 3 hours.

TO SERVE, place 4–6 footed glass goblets in the refrigerator 10–15 minutes before serving. Spoon the granita into the chilled goblets. Garnish with mint sprigs and orange zest strips, if desired. Serve immediately. ☙

Pear Sorbet

Here's another recipe developed to make in the new home electric ice cream machines.

Make a syrup by dissolving ³/₄ cup (6 oz) sugar in 1 cup water. Measure out ¹/₄ cup (2 fl oz) of the syrup and place in a small bowl with the juice of 1 lemon. Stir well. Halve, core and peel 4 pears, then cut into small pieces. Immediately put the pear pieces into the syrup–lemon juice mixture and stir to coat well. In a food processor fitted with the metal blade, purée the pear-syrup mixture, in batches if necessary. Transfer to a large bowl and add the remaining syrup and 1 tablespoon kirsch or pear-flavored liqueur. Freeze immediately in an ice cream maker according to the manufacturer's instructions. This sorbet cannot be kept for more than 1 day as it will gradually turn brown. Makes about 1 ¹/₂ quart.

WHILE A PARTICULAR PERSON OR INCIDENT can often be cited as the reason for a specific change in a country's cuisine, the true story behind the evolution of how people cook is much more complex. Over the past 40 years, countless people beyond those already named in this book have influenced what we cook, the way we cook and how we eat. I would like to acknowledge some of them here, but with the clear understanding that it would take many, many pages to list everyone who deserves mention.

Hundreds of authors have given us cookbooks that helped to change our everyday cooking habits, with James Beard, Julia Child and Marcella Hazan among the most influential. None of these books would have been offered to us without the hard work of cookbook editors, chief among them Judith Jones of Alfred A. Knopf.

Restaurants have also made an impact. The introduction of French cuisine to the United States in this century began at the 1939 World's Fair in New York, where both the French and Belgian pavilions set up first-rate, immensely popular restaurants. Following the close of the fair, Henri Soulé, chef at the French pavilion, opened the great Le Pavillon in New York, which led to a proliferation of grand French restaurants—Chambord, La Caravelle, Lutèce—in that city after World War II.

Over the years, new ideas came from scores of restaurant owners and chefs, among them Alice Waters of Chez Panisse in Berkeley; Jeremiah Tower of Stars and Joyce Goldstein of Square One in San Francisco; Alfredo Viazzi of Alfredo's Trattoria and Leon Lianides of The Coach House in New York; Rene Verdon, the famed White House chef; and Joseph Baum of Restaurant Associates, who opened such trendsetting establishments as La Fonda del Sol, Four Seasons, and Windows on the World.

Cooking schools sprang up everywhere and educated us to be better cooks. Among the teachers who made a difference were Mary Risely and her Tante Marie Cooking School in San Francisco, Julie Dannenbaum in Philadelphia and Mexican cooking expert Diana Kennedy. The Culinary Institute of America, founded in New York in 1946, was turning out chefs every year, many of whom went on to become household names. In Paris, La Varenne Cooking School was attracting American professional and home cooks and training them in classic French cuisine.

Food journalists and restaurant critics kept us up-to-date on the latest trends. Two journalists of particular note were William Rice of The Washington Post and the Chicago Tribune, and Helen McCully of McCalls and House Beautiful. Among the top critics who advised us on where to eat were Mimi Sheraton, Craig Claiborne and Gael Greene, all of them New York based but with national reputations. During these decades, cooking magazines kept us current, too, with Gourmet, Bon Appétit, and House & Garden the leaders.

It was the new specialty-food shops, however, that brought us the products that inspired us. Two of the most important operations were Dean and Deluca and The Silver Palate. The latter's founders, Sheila Lukins and Julee Rosso, went on to write The Silver Palate cookbook, a national best seller. Needless to say, wine was also developing a following, and Sam Aaron of Sherry Wine & Spirits in New York and Robert Mondavi in Napa were leading voices in how to match wine with food.

Finally, there were the countless equipment manufacturers who helped to mold the way Americans cook. Two central figures were Ron Kasperzak, the man behind Calphalon cookware, and Carl Sontheimer, who brought us the Cuisinart food processor. It has been a wonderful 40 years of changes, and I am glad I was part of it.

Chuck Williams

CREDITS & ACKNOWLEDGMENTS

Even though I swept the sidewalk and mopped the floor every morning, it was Mike Sharp and Wade Bentson who contributed so much to the success of Williams-Sonoma during those first 20 years. A few years later, Howard Lester and Pat Connolly came on board and steered Williams-Sonoma on its remarkable course of change and growth during its last two decades. I also salute the thousands of dedicated Williams-Sonoma employees, both past and present, who have contributed so much to our success. Without them, there would be no 40th anniversary to celebrate.

I would like to thank Jim Stirratt for pursuing the production of this work, Elaine Anderson for her help in handling the mountains of material needed for its realization, and the skillful design and editorial staff of Weldon Owen for producing a memorable book, especially Hannah Rahill, Norman Kolpas and Kari Perin, who pulled it all together.

Weldon Owen, Inc. would like to thank the Jack Morton Agency for organizing and photographing memorabilia from the private collections of Chuck Williams and Williams-Sonoma, and Elaine Anderson, Katherine Withers Cobbs and Cecily Upton for their assistance and support.

PHOTOGRAPHY
Acknowledgment is made for all photographs not taken specifically for the purpose of this work: People Weekly c. 1982 Michael Alexander, page 92 (bottom right); Allan Rosenberg, page 134 (bottom left); Chris Shorten, page 5; from the collection of Chuck Williams, page 9 (top left); 9 (top middle); 9 (top right); 92 (top left).

QUOTATIONS
Weldon Owen Inc. gratefully acknowledges all the authors of quotations used herein. We would particularly like to thank the following publishers for permission to use excerpts from the following works: From *The Classic Italian Cook Book,* by Marcella Hazan. Copyright © 1976 by Marcella Hazan. Reprinted courtesy of Alfred A. Knopf. From *Entertaining,* by Martha Stewart. Copyright © 1982 by Martha Stewart. Reprinted by permission of Clarkson N. Potter, a division of Crown Publishers, Inc. From *The Foods and Wine of Spain,* by Penelope Casas. Copyright © 1983 by Penelope Casas. Reprinted courtesy of Alfred A. Knopf. From Foods of the World, *The Cooking of Italy,* by Waverley Root and the Editors of Time-Life Books. Copyright © 1968 by Time Inc. From Foods of the World, *The Cooking of Provincial France,* by M.F.K. Fisher and the Editors of Time-Life Books. Copyright © 1968 by Time Inc. From *Season to Taste,* by Peggy Harvey. Copyright © 1960 by Peggy Harvey. Reprinted courtesy of Alfred A. Knopf.

RECIPES
The recipes in this book have been compiled from early Williams-Sonoma catalogs, the original *Williams-Sonoma Cookbook and Guide to Kitchenware* (©1986 by Williams-Sonoma, Inc.), and two volumes from the Chuck Williams Collection *Simple Italian Cooking* (© 1995 by Weldon Owen, Inc.) and *Simple French Cooking* (© 1996 by Weldon Owen, Inc.).